PALACES

PALACES

DAVID ROSS

MetroBooks

MetroBooks

An Imprint of Friedman/Fairfax Publishers

©1998 by Michael Friedman Publishing Group, Inc.

Library of Congress Cataloging-in-Publication Data available upon request.

ISBN 1-56799-472-5

Color separations by Lydia Litho, London
Printed in England by Butler & Tanner Limited

Editor: Lydia Darbyshire
Designer: Zoë Mellors
Picture Researcher: International Image Select

Commissioned, designed, and produced by Haldane Mason Ltd, London

Frontispiece: Palace of Versailles, France
Opposite: Interior, the Doge's Palace, Venice
Overleaf: The Alhambra Palace, Granada, Spain

For bulk purchases and special sales, please contact:
Friedman/Fairfax Publishers
Attention: Sales Department
15 West 26th Street
New York, NY 10010
212/685-6610 FAX 212/685-1307

Visit our website:
http://www.metrobooks.com

Dedication

THIS BOOK IS DEDICATED TO THE SPIRIT OF JOHN RUSKIN,

WHO SAW THE INHERENT POETRY OF ARCHITECTURE,

WHETHER IN COTTAGE OR PALACE.

Contents

The history of the
PALACE

The word palace comes from the Latin word *palatium*. The Palatine Hill in Rome – *mons palatinus* in Latin – was the first of the Seven Hills to be settled and fortified. When the Roman Empire was established, the first emperor, Augustus (reigned 27BC–AD14), had his home there. So the house of the Palatine became a byword for the house of the emperor. Eventually, as rulers called themselves tsar or kaiser, in imitation of Caesar, so their houses were known as palaces. Later still, the word came also to mean the great house of a nobleman, such as the Duke of Marlborough's Blenheim Palace in England. Today, the word can be applied to any grand, stately building, or any building that aspires to be so. Thus the glass and iron exhibition hall of Victorian London was called the Crystal Palace, and countless cinemas ran up columns on the front and became picture palaces.

Schönbrunn Palace, Vienna, Austria

Developed from a sixteenth-century hunting lodge, the palace as we see it today originated in 1696. The baroque architect Fischer von Erlach (1656–1723) planned it to outdo Versaille, but even the Habsburg resources were insufficient for this. From 1740 it became the summer palace of the Empress Maria Theresa.

Of course, there were palaces long before Rome. While half-wild sheep and goats still grazed on the Palatine Hill, the great civilizations of the Middle and Far East were flourishing. Through the centuries, however, the word "palace" has meant not just a stately building, but one with an additional function — the business of ruling, of government. Some palaces, like the Elysée in Paris, remain centers of executive power. Others, like Amalienborg in Copenhagen, are emblematic only, the residence of a democratic monarch. The word retains its principal meaning — the main residence of the country's chief citizen — and it is found in most Western languages, from the French *palais*, to the German *Palast*, from the Dutch *paleis*, to the Italian *palazzo*. There is a further significance attached to the word. A palace is not fortified. If it is turned into a stronghold, it becomes a castle or a fortress and ceases to be a palace. Palaces imply if not necessarily peace, at least government and some sort of stability.

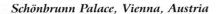

Schönbrunn Palace, Vienna, Austria

Schönbrunn's splendid park is French baroque in style, laid out symmetrically by Jean Trehet in 1705, although remodeled somewhat in the 1760s. The name means "beautiful fountains," and springs still feed the fountains in the grounds.

Pavlosk Palace, near Tsarskoe Selo, Russia

Above: The St. Petersburg region of Russia is rich in palaces. The son of Empress Catherine the Great, the future Tsar Paul I, built "Paul's Palace" in 1787. He was assassinated in 1801.

Right: The superb state bedroom, with painted silk hangings and a chandelier from the Imperial Glass Factory.

The house of the sovereign was much more than a home. It was the main office of the government. It was the high court of law. It was where the monarch was on view and gave audience to his or her own subjects and to ambassadors and travelers from other lands. Consequently, it was built and decorated to display the wealth of the realm and the magnificence of the sovereign.

Even in the earliest eras of human life, it is likely that the dwelling of the headman was distinguished from those of his tribespeople. Nomadic and pastoral groups, living in makeshift or portable accommodation, made a greater hut or tent for him, and placed it either centrally or at a respectful distance. In the Middle Ages, the tented palace of Attila the Hun was fabled for its vast size and luxury. Palaces have always been places of fascination, the home of a favored few, places of luxury, of splendor, of debauchery — and of danger. "The great man's house has slippery seats," says an ancient proverb. For palaces, too, had their dungeons and secret rooms, where fallen favorites might spend long, solitary years or meet sudden and violent death.

CHAPTER ONE

FROM THE

First Civilizations to Roman

SPLENDOR

EGYPT

Ancient Egypt provides the oldest surviving remnants of palaces. Here perhaps began the tradition that the palace was not the most grand of buildings. The temple was grander still. In Egypt, the pharaoh was seen as a living god, and the temple, where he spoke to the other gods, was regarded as more important than the house in which the pharaoh lived. The temple was made of stone; the palace was made of bricks and wood, with decorative stone features at its entrance.

The pharaoh had two palaces — one in Lower Egypt by the Nile delta and one in Upper Egypt — and they were by far the finest houses in the kingdom. The most important of the public apartments was a great hall, in which the pharaoh might receive his subjects and from the front door of which, on a high throne, he would dispense justice. Next in importance was the room in which great feasts would be given. These were elaborate occasions, with many courses, music, and dancing to entertain the diners. Accommodation was provided for the storage of treasure, weapons, clothing, and for the supervising officials, such as the Director of the Pharaoh's Dress. Libraries and muniment rooms kept the records of the state. Private apartments, particularly the women's quarters, were barred to the outsider. Also part of the same complex of buildings were the kitchen, bakehouse, and brewhouse. The garden, with trellises and a pool, was intended as a cool haven in the heat of the sun. These are all features of the palace that will recur time and again. The Egyptian palace was a low building, probably no more than two floors high, but spreading over a wide area. There was one great exception — the Ramesseum at Thebes — a vast and imposing palace-cum-mortuary temple erected by the pharaoh Rameses II (1279– 1213BC). The palace elements are an audience chamber, throne room, and private apartments. From here, a pylon gateway, flanked by two colossal statues, leads up to the sanctuary. In the palaces that catered to their earthly existences, pharaohs of the New Kingdom period (1550–1069BC) installed very basic washrooms next to their sleeping apartments. They also laid out great parks. In the case of Amenophis III (1390–1352BC) the park around his palace near Thebes was large enough to include a lake on which he sailed in his royal yacht, *Splendor of the Aten*.

Nineveh, Iraq

The reconstruction of the Ishtar Gate, Babylon, from c.575BC.

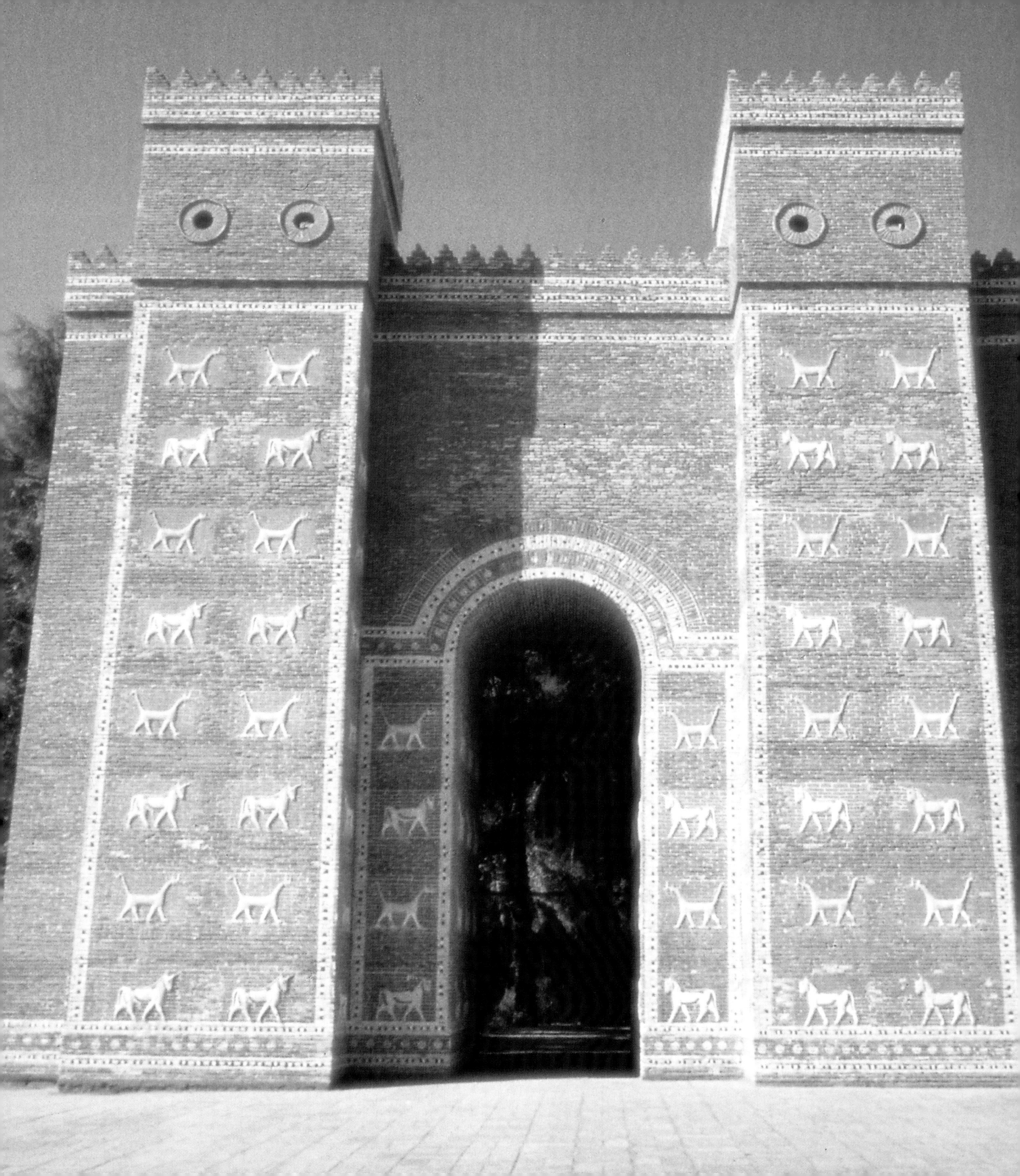

Layard (1817–1894) uncovered them. Twenty-eight rooms were opened, showing reliefs, painted ornaments, frescoes, friezes of men, castles, ships, animals, and massive sculptures. Khorsabad also shows arched doorways and wall pilasters that seem to foreshadow Greek buildings yet to come.

CRETE

Secure against attack thanks to their naval strength, the island rulers of Crete constructed splendid palaces in the period 1900–1300BC. The famous palace of Knossos shows a superb adaptation of a sloping site to create a grand stairway, rising through four flights. This was a large building for display, entertainment, and worship. It was a sacred place, and the visitor would have undergone rites of purification before entering. Its western side contains the ceremonial rooms, including a throne room with a stone throne flanked by painted griffins and a sunken basin.

It is more likely, though, that the Hall of the Double Axes, on the east side, was where the king sat to give audience. This hall is illuminated and aired by light-wells (unroofed areas), just as the palaces of ancient America were. The central court, with its famous bull-leaping fresco, was the arena for this practice, half-ritual, half-sport. The Minoans equipped their palaces with washrooms, drained by pipes of terra cotta. The lower rooms were used for the storage

ASSYRIA

The palaces of Assyria were made of clay brick, and their architectural style is hard to reconstruct from the heaps that remain. One of the best preserved, that of King Sargon (reigned 721–705BC) at Khorsabad (Dur-Sharrukin), dating from 720BC, has a great courtyard and several smaller ones, with halls and rooms arranged irregularly around the outer walls. These actually form the base of a huge platform, 4920 feet (1500 meters) across, on which the complex is built. Its walls were straight and plain,

faced with thin cement or a screed of stone, and topped by battlements.

Any decoration was confined to the sculptural ornaments, and these were splendid and imposing. Magnificent winged bulls and lions, designed to flank processional doorways, were found when the featureless site of ancient Nineveh was excavated. Destroyed 700 years before the Christian era, the palace of Nineveh kept its treasures until the nineteenth century, when the British archaeologist Sir Austen Henry

Persepolis, Iran

Left: The staircase from Persepolis, with a frieze of warriors carved in relief.

Right: A monumental doorway from Persepolis, showing the influence of Egyptian "pylon" gateways.

of corn, oil, and wine, and the great jars may still be seen. Around 1375BC the great palace of Knossos burned to the ground, whether by accident or design is not known.

PERSIA

Two centuries after Sargon arose the empire first of the Medes, then of the Persians. More survives of their structures because they made greater use of solid stonework.

The assimilative Persians picked up various styles as their empire spread. The superb palaces of Cyrus II, the Great (c.585BC–c.529BC) at Pasargadae and of Darius I, the Great (reigned 522BC–486BC) at Persepolis are built, like Assyrian palaces, on great platforms 50 feet (15 meters) above the ground. Persepolis has winged bulls guarding doorways and Assyrian-style sculptures of lion hunts on its great stairway. But the columned halls of Persepolis clearly show that the architects had also learned from their conquest of Egypt and such columned temple halls as those of Karnak. However, the Persian roofs were of timber, and the pillars consequently more slender, so that the whole edifice avoid the solemn gloom of the Egyptian interior.

PALACES OF THE ANCIENT WORLD

The first palaces may have been built in Ancient Egypt more than five thousand years ago. A great palace existed at Knossos, in the island of Crete, while over many centuries the Middle East saw powerful rulers build palaces — notably those at Khorsabad, Nineveh, and Persepolis. This ancient tradition of large-scale building foreshadowed classical Greek and Roman architecture.

GREECE AND ROME

For all their somewhat barbaric splendor, the palaces of the ancient Middle East did not influence later builders in other lands. But as Persia declined, a new and dynamic power overcame her to rule most of the known world — the mainland Greeks.

Greek architecture had a profound influence on the Western world, but the type of building on which the Greeks lavished their ingenuity was the temple. The network of warlike and warring city-states housed its

rulers in citadels for safety. But often there was no king and no need for a palace. Ever distrustful of tyrants, self-governing Greek communities such as Athens showed their civic pride by constructing temples, of which the Parthenon is the most splendid, to house their patron god or goddess.

Although they did not build palaces, the Greeks provided later architects with the elements with which palaces would be designed. They established stone as the material for stately buildings. They worked

Tivoli, Rome, Italy

The colonnade from Hadrian's villa at Tivoli (second century AD).

out the ratio of one part to another, so that any building, no matter how large or small, was in proportion. For centuries the Greek-style pediment would define the palace throughout the world.

The immediate inheritors of the Greek tradition were the Romans. By the second

Livia's Villa, Prima Porta, Rome, Italy

This wall-painting, depicting an elegant terrace overlooking verdant countryside, is from the Empress Livia's country house — if not a palace, then at least an example of Roman aristocratic gracious living.

century BC they had conquered Greece, where they came under the influence of Greek culture. They already employed the rounded arch, and to this they added the orders, beams, and colonnades of Greece. But the Romans had a taste for monumentality. Their capital city, in the days of the empire, was vaster than any Greek town. They developed the apartment block and the use of concrete, and they built huge buildings as temples, assembly rooms, and public baths. There was no king: the seat of government was the senate house.

In comparison, even the great private houses were unostentatious, not more than two floors high and built around a central atrium. But the Romans were the first people to achieve domestic comfort. They had sophisticated heating, a water supply, and drainage. Walls and floors were decorated with mosaic tiling, and there were wall paintings and comfortable furniture.

Augustus's house on the Palatine Hill was relatively modest. However, a significant change took place with his successors, whose palaces had no public function. The first emperor to build for sheer opulence was Nero (reigned 54–68), whose fabulous Golden House was a sprawling pleasure palace designed to underline his personal supremacy and to provide the most luxurious accommodation the world had yet seen. With the fall of Nero, the Golden House was utterly destroyed, but a more

tasteful reminder of the empire is found in Hadrian's villa at Tivoli, outside Rome. Hadrian (reigned 117–138) was a great admirer of Greek art, and the palatial country retreat of Tivoli shows a brilliant blend of the Roman genius for landscaping and engineering with the subtle elegance of Greek styling.

The seat of the empire was moving east. In the fourth century AD, the Emperor Diocletian (reigned 284–305) organized the erection of an enormous palace at Spalato (Split) on the eastern Adriatic coast. Far more than a residence or even an imperial office, the complex was designed to house the vast entourage with which the emperor was surrounded — secretaries, the Praetorian Guard, officials, courtiers, servants. It included a temple, and an octagonal rotunda, probably planned as the emperor's mausoleum. This building displays novelties of style: notably, arcades of arches are found springing directly from the capitals of the columns and supporting the upper parts of the wall. Before this, the Greek entablature had always been employed.

CHAPTER TWO

THE PALACES OF

Medieval

EUROPE

After the final collapse of Rome in 455 there was only one city in Europe where a palace could safely be built, and that was Constantinople, in the eastern corner. For a millennium it would be a source of wonder and rumor to the rest of the world. Today, almost nothing remains of the awesome palaces built there by successive dynasties, other than the empty site of the Blachernae Palace and the remarkable cisterns built to supply water to the Great Palace of Justinian.

Western Europe did not see a new palace until *c*.790, when the Frankish king Charles, who became the Emperor Charlemagne in 800, built his new palace at Aachen (begun 792). It consisted of two buildings joined by a colonnade. One was a great Sala Regalis, or throne room, built like a Roman basilica with the throne set in the apse; the other was the Palatine Chapel. Built in a conscious spirit of Roman revival, these Carolingian buildings anticipated the Romanesque style. The Sala Regalis is gone, but the Palatine Chapel remains, its two-story octagon a signal to the pagan world that the old skills of the western empire had not entirely died out.

Early medieval Europe did not create many more palaces, however, for this was the era of the development of the keep, and then the fortified castle. Monarchs and other rulers required stout walls and the ability to withstand sieges rather than a sumptuous display. In Scotland, where feudal warfare was still rife, a little Renaissance palace was erected within the windswept but secure walls of Stirling Castle.

The Doge's Palace, Venice, Italy

The fourteenth-century front that overlooks the Bacino di San Marco and the entrance to the Grand Canal is a superb example of late Gothic design.

The Doge's Palace, Venice, Italy

Imposing from without and within, the Doge's Palace (far left) proclaimed Venetian mastery of the sea, while visitors to the doge's court were intended to be overawed by crushingly ornate interiors such as the Sala del Anti-collegio (left).

PALACES AFTER ROME'S FALL

After the fifth-century break-up of the Roman Empire in the west, Europe fell into decay. Civilization and learning returned under the ninth-century emperor Charlemagne, "Charles the Great", whose palace at Aachen was a university as well as a seat of government. In the east the Roman Empire continued, with splendid palaces at Constantinople, formerly Byzantium. Meanwhile, Venice grew rich and powerful on trade with the East.

VENICE

One place where it seemed safe to establish a palace was in the city-state of Venice, secure on its islands in the Adriatic Sea. The first palace of the doges was begun in 814, on the same site as its successor, at the end of the Grand Canal. Its present aspect dates from the first half of the fifteenth century, when the superb Gothic front facing the Piazzetta was completed, and although much work was done subsequently, the palace still preserves the sense of a Gothic building with Renaissance features and decoration. It was damaged by fire in 1483, after which Antonio Rizzo (c.1430–99) created the east façade of the great courtyard and the Scala dei Giganti, which rises to the piano nobile, or second floor. The doges were crowned on the landing.

The Scala d'Oro, built in 1538–58 by Scapagnano, at the direction of Jacopo Sansovino (1486–1570), leads to the third and fourth floors. On the fourth floor is the Sala del Collegio, with its tribune (gallery) where the College of Councilors sat with the doge, and a magnificent range of paintings by Tintoretto (Jacopo Robusti, c.1518–94) and Paolo Veronese (Paolo Caliari, 1528–88), including Veronese's ceiling depicting Justice and Peace making offerings to Venice. The Sala del Maggior Consiglio (begun 1340), long said to be the largest room in Italy, contains historical paintings by Venetian masters and the great frieze of doges' portraits by Tintoretto and his pupils. In Tintoretto's *Paradise*, it also holds the largest oil painting in the world, 23 x 72 feet (7 x 22 meters). After these superb but intimidating chambers, the doge's private apartments are a surprise — three small rooms. Of course, the doge was simply the figurehead, representing the splendor of the state, but it is notable how often the rulers' private rooms are comparatively simple, like those of Philip II in the vast Escorial near Madrid and those of the Emperor Franz Josef in the mighty Hofburg of Vienna.

Ca' d'Oro, Venice, Italy

Further up the Grand Canal there rose from 1425 the most beautiful Gothic façade in Venice, the front of the Ca' d'Oro. Commissioned by Marco Contarini, and the work of Matteo Raverti and Giovanni Bon or Buon (c.1355–1443) and his brother Bartolomeo (c.1374–1467), its delicate stone tracery was originally gilded, whence its name, the Golden House. The courtyard is the finest in Venice, with the well-head being Bon's masterpiece. The Ca' d'Oro was restored in 1895 and again in the 1970s and 1980s, and it is now a museum with a fine collection of paintings, sculptures, medals, ceramics, and furniture. The finest of its kind, it is representative of many hundreds of palazzi in the cities of Italy, created for powerful local families who were not rulers but who used their wealth for the beauty of their city as well as for the display of their own culture and position.

CHAPTER THREE

PALACE CULTURES

of the

AMERICAS

For three thousand years, in Central and South America, civilizations rose and fell before the vast land-mass was ever "discovered" by explorers venturing from Europe. Without the aid of metal tools or the wheel there arose a succession of cities, laid out with geometric and astronomical precision, dominated by great, stepped pyramidal structures, and filled with temples, plazas, and palaces. It was an architecture of display, concerned with the outside rather than with the interior — a fit setting for procession and ritual.

TIKAL

At the same time as imperial Rome was flourishing, a vast city existed at Tikal. In the lush green lowlands of Central America, in what is today Guatemala, this Mayan city spread for miles around its ceremonial center in a pattern of forest, fields, buildings, and farms. Its palaces, emblems of this great and sophisticated civilization, were tall buildings, five stories or more, but this, too, was an architecture of external display, and the inner rooms of the palaces are small and dark, linked by tall corridors with vaulted ceilings.

Imposing as they are, they show that the lives of the individual inhabitants were not regarded as important — as in ancient Egypt, it was their function that counted, and that was exercised outside the palace. A typical part of the Mayan and most other Meso-American temple-plaza-palace complexes

Teotihuacán, Mexico

The city covers some 7³/₄ square miles (20 km²), and its population was around 150,000. Cortés and his band passed close to the buried site without suspecting its existence.

A thousand years before Columbus, priest-kings ruled in Mexico from huge palace and temple complexes near modern Mexico City. This was Teotihuacán, a name ("place of the gods") given by the Aztecs to the ruins they discovered centuries later. Elsewhere, the Mayan peoples of southern Mexico created further wealthy palace centres at Tikal and Palenque. For nearly three millennia, empires flourished in South and Central America, culminating in the awesome wealth and power of the Aztec emperor Moctezuma II, whose palace at Tenochtitlán was pillaged by the Spanish under Cortés.

was the ball-court. This stone enclosure or sunken court, invariably richly decorated with a carved frieze, could be from 100 to 200 feet (30–60 meters) long, and was rectangular in shape, with the goals at the narrow ends. Like everything else in Mayan life, it had a religious dimension, which did not prevent intense gambling. The game itself was amazingly dexterous, since players were not allowed to use hands, arms, or feet to touch the ball.

PALENQUE

Perhaps the classic Mayan city is Palenque, in Chiapas, Mexico, and among its superb ruins stands the great complex of buildings known as the Palace, which dates from the seventh century. The architects here had learned how to build with more slender walls that created a delicate effect, and an interior design that gave greater air and space. The Palace, which is built up on a square-shaped artificial base, is reached by a ceremonial flight of steps, divided into three sets of nine, and its buildings are formed around four inner patios. Its most striking feature is the tower, unique in pre-Columbian architecture and almost Oriental in its appearance. It probably had the dual function of watch-tower and observatory. The Palace of Palenque is full of fascinating detail. Wall niches and small T-shaped windows hint at functions that can only be guessed at. There is an almost-Moorish carved archway. The limestone steps and walls are finely carved in bas-relief or covered with stucco ornamentation that was painted in many colors. In its heyday the Palace must have been stunning.

MITLA

West of Palenque, in what is now Oaxaca, Mexico, and some 300 years later, the Mixtec-Zapotec peoples constructed the

Palenque, Mexico

The name is Spanish, meaning "barriers of sticks." The eastern half of the site, with the Palace, covering over a third of a square mile (about one square kilometer), is the best preserved. The western sector, almost as large again, is mostly unrestored.

Teotihuacán, Mexico

The pyramids of the Sun and Moon dominating the central area. (first century AD).

sacred city of Mitla. Its Palace of the Columns is clearly a courtly building. The broad antechamber, with a roof supported by six monolithic columns, leads into a complex of four rooms set around a great rectangular central hall. It is easy to imagine a throned priest-king in a gorgeously feathered cloak giving audience while a group of awed supplicants waits in the anteroom, ignored by guards and acolytes.

What is most striking about the Palace of the Columns, apart from its clarity of design, is the remarkable workmanship in stone achieved by a people who had neither bronze nor iron tools. Not only is it cut with extreme precision, but it is also carved in a great variety of abstract patterns. Set in panel form between the finely jointed cornerstones, the carvings turn the external walls into virtuoso lacework.

TEOTIHUACÁN

Teotihuacán ("place of the gods" — a name bestowed on the already-ruined site by the Aztecs), stands in Mexico's central plateau northeast of present-day Mexico City. At its peak (AD450–AD650), it was a teeming metropolis of religion and commerce, ruled by priest-kings. At its ceremonial center is the Palace of Quetzalpapálotl, or Quetzal-butterfly, probably the residence of a high priest. In this city of temple-pyramids, those of the Sun and Moon dominate, while the palace was a low, richly decorated structure, built around a largely restored central patio. On three sides it opens into spacious rooms; on the fourth it gives access to adjacent buildings. The carved pillars display the butterfly motif that gives the palace its name. On their inner side are stone rings, which once secured the curtains that ran behind, acting as doors and windows and reducing the fierce contrast between the bright sunlight and the dark interiors. This was a residence and not a place of ceremonial, but its calm severity of design and its size make it plain that here was a seat of power and authority, and it is easy to visualize the stately procession that would escort its occupant from here to the temple where, in the complete integration of religion and daily life, his court would be held, his judgments given, and his sacrifices performed.

To the southwest, in the heart of a residential area, is the handsome Palace of Zacuala, which is believed to have been the residence of a great merchant or high official. Surrounded by narrow streets, it opens into a broad pattern of airy courts and wide chambers. These courts, varying in size from the vast central patio to simple light-wells, were essential to give the windowless building light and air. Three large reception chambers open on to the great patio, and the building has its own west-facing temple. Only fragmentary remains now exist of the brilliant frescoes that once decorated the inner walls of these buildings — figures of gods and animals, depicting a jungle paradise full of flowers and butterflies.

TENOCHTITLÁN

By far the greatest palace of ancient America was that of the Aztec emperor Moctezuma II in his capital of Tenochtitlán, today, Mexico City. Here, the palace dominated even the temple structures. Nothing of either remains, and only the awestruck accounts of the Spaniards who invaded in 1521 help us to imagine the splendor of these palaces rising from gardens, canals, and lakes: "How large and well built they were, of excellent stonework, and the wood of cedars and other good sweet-smelling trees, with great courts and rooms — everything all very whitewashed and shining, with so many kinds of stones and paintings on them that one would never tire of gazing on them," wrote Bernal Diaz del Castillo, a soldier in Cortés's army. He added: "Now all is razed, nothing remains!"

CHAPTER FOUR

FROM URBINO TO VERSAILLES:

The Renaissance PALACE

During the fifteenth century, the rise in power and wealth of the city of Florence in northern Italy produced the desire among its inhabitants to make it the most beautiful place in Europe. In a curious way, by ignoring the flamboyant Gothic style that was all the rage elsewhere in Europe and by looking instead into the Italian past, they produced an artistic and architectural revolution that would change the appearance of every city in the continent. The architects Filippo Brunelleschi (1377–1446), who was responsible for the dome of Florence Cathedral, and Leon Battista Alberti (1404–72), were at the heart of this movement. Alberti, in fact, wrote the first architectural book of the Renaissance, *De re aedificatoria* (1452), and in the façade of the Palazzo Rucellai in Florence (1446–70) he incorporated pilasters for the first time in domestic architecture.

ITALY

Urbino

No palace anywhere shows the ideas and ideals of the Renaissance more clearly than that begun by the duke of Urbino, in northeastern Italy, in 1447. When the architect Luciano Laurana (*c.*1420–79) was appointed in 1467, the new Palazzo Ducale became a marvel of its times. Although it still occupied the old hilltop site, its big windows and open loggias open up the curtain walls to show a grand house rather than a fortress. There is no towering keep, only a level roof-line. Envious or admiring patrons, including Lorenzo de' Medici, asked for plans and drawings so that they could emulate or try to surpass it. The spirit behind the palace was Federico di Montefeltro (1422–82), humanist, soldier, scholar, and patron of art. It was on his

Ducal Palace, Urbino, Italy

Described as "the first royal palace of modern times," Urbino had libraries, a theater, a riding school, a mausoleum, a greenhouse, two bathrooms, and an ice house.

The first building has two-lighted windows in the Florentine style, and Laurano's block, with its unfinished marble facing, adjoins it. The capitals above the pillars in the great courtyard show the purity of early Renaissance carving; their motifs are repeated on the pilasters that rise from architrave to cornice, between two bands of inscriptions outlining the duke's virtuous qualities. A monumental staircase, one of the first of its kind, rises to the piano nobile. Inside, the apartments of the duke and duchess have delicate carving around doors, windows, and chimney-pieces.

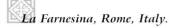

La Farnesina, Rome, Italy.

The Farnese family, one of Italy's grandest and a source of cardinals and popes, was well endowed with splendid houses. This is the grand hall of La Farnesina, the epitome of a Renaissance palace and decorated in appropriate splendor.

court that Castiglione modeled the courtly ideal in his book *Il cortegiano* (*The Courtier*), which became Europe's guide to a new level of civilized behavior.

The Sala degli Angeli has Ambrogio Barocci's angel sculptures, colored gold and blue. The door between this and the throne room has intarsia work by Sandro Botticelli (*c*.1445–1510), whose work is also seen in the studiolo, the Duke's tiny, exquisite study with a desk and chair that fold back into the paneling. It shows one of the earliest and most complete examples of *trompe l'oeil*, or illusionism, painting in Italy. Every inch is used for shelves, cupboards, and paintings. Above the intarsia paneling, a frieze of great men from Moses to Petrarch gaze down. The little room is windowless, but leads out to a loggia from which a superb view extends over the rugged countryside. The duchess' salon has a fine vaulted ceiling painted by Francesco de Giorgio (1439–1502), and successive visitors have noted that the careful duke had placed a handle only on the outer side of her bedroom door.

In 1626, Urbino passed into the hands of Pope Urban VIII, who removed most of its treasures. In the following century, it was home to the Old Pretender, James Edward Stuart, claimant to the British throne, and his Jacobite court in exile. Now it houses the National Gallery of the Marche province.

Rome

A generation of brilliant men in Italy, of whom Donato Bramante (1444–1514), Leonardo da Vinci (1452–1519), and Michelangelo Buonarotti (1475–1564), were the most notable, developed the forms and ideas of the early Renaissance and created many masterpieces. With zest, energy, and a spirit of emulation, they were determined that each new building would show some progress.

Rome, with its college of cardinals, each of whom required his own palatial residence, became a building site. Here, in 1516, Raphael (1483–1520) began the Villa Madama for Cardinal de' Medici, with its great garden loggia, derived from the recently unearthed remains of Nero's Golden House. In 1517, Antonio da Sangallo the Younger (1483–1546) began the Palazzo Farnese, perhaps the quintessential palace of the High Renaissance, enlarged to its present monumental but perfectly balanced grandeur when its owner became Pope Paul III in 1534 (the great cornice was added by Michelangelo in the 1540s). Baldassare Peruzzi (1481–

1536) built the Palazzo Massimi in 1532; its irregularly curved frontage represents an act of architectural daring whose revolutionary impact is hard now to imagine. And from 1549, Andrea Palladio (1508–80) was at work. His open-looking, airy palace buildings, like the Villa Barbaro of 1560, make free use of Greek themes, with tall columns and pediments, but combine them with arches, domes, and curves. The Palladian style was especially perfect for country palaces, and his influence on palace architecture was very long-lived.

RENAISSANCE ITALY

During the Renaissance, Italy regained a cultural and economic influence in Europe that recalled something of Roman times. Florence and Venice were the most powerful of a number of city states dominated by immensely wealthy families such as the Medici of Florence, whose grip extended to the leadership of the Roman Catholic Church itself. Dynamic merchant princes built sumptuous palaces in imitation of the rediscovered Roman and Greek civilizations, while in Rome equally dynamic cardinals and popes set about recreating the greatness of classical Rome. Across the Alps, kings and emperors were inspired by the Italian Renaissance to build palaces of their own.

The Pitti Palace, Florence, Italy

Left: Fresco from the Grand Duke's throne room, by the Mannerists Agostino Mitelli (1609–60) and Angelo Michele Colonna (1600–87).

Above: The garden front, showing the use of rustication — the deeply incised and separated stone blockwork — to create a dramatic effect of light and shade, and also to contrast its stern solidity with the airy apertures of the arches and windows.

Florence

From Urbino, the duke was content to look out over a grand vista. On the more level ground of Florence, the Pitti Palace was to combine building and gardens in a unity. It was begun for Luca Pitti, a rich citizen, by Brunelleschi, but work stopped when Pitti fell into disgrace. In 1549 it was acquired by Eleanor, wife of Cosimo I de' Medici, who

also inaugurated work on the Boboli Gardens (named after the Boboli, who had owned some of the land) behind it. It became the residence of the grand dukes of Tuscany. A balustrade replaced the old roof, and Bartolomeo Ammanati (1511–92) inserted Renaissance windows (c.1568) into the blank ground-floor arches. Ammanati was also responsible for the courtyard and garden front. Work went on into the seventeenth century with the addition of the wings (1620–31) and the end annexes (1764), and continued into the nineteenth century.

On the garden front, the quadrangular form was not brought above the ground-floor level so as to integrate the palace and garden. Successive grand dukes embellished the gardens with fountains and statues. One of the most charming features is the Isolotto, the "little island," with its bridges, statuary, flowers, and lemon trees. King Victor

Emmanuel III (reigned 1900–46) presented the Pitti Palace to the nation in 1919, and it is now one of the world's greatest art galleries, with a collection that includes such paintings as Titian's portrait of Pietro Aretino, which is very much at home, since it was presented by the sitter to Cosimo I.

FRANCE

Reports, books, drawings, and talented pupils helped to spread the new concepts across Europe and as far as America, which had been bumped into by Christopher Columbus in 1492 on his way, as he thought, to the East Indies. But the first, and most fertile, ground on which the seeds fell was France. A rich kingdom, with wealthy dukedoms and church estates, France also held a host of artists who responded eagerly to the stimulus from Italy. The first French Renaissance buildings, the (now destroyed) chateau of Gaillon near Rouen and the Loire chateaux of Blois and Chambord, show an attractive marriage of late-medieval French silhouette and pure Renaissance detail.

RENAISSANCE EUROPE

Outside Italy, Renaissance Europe's states, princedoms, and kingdoms were becoming wealthy and prosperous. Only in resolutely democratic Switzerland was there a capital city without a palace. Elsewhere, there were ducal, royal, and imperial palaces, centers of pomp and circumstance, with parading soldiers, court flunkeys, and gilded carriages waiting in the stables.

Chateau de Chambord, France

This magnificent building was begun by François I in 1519, but construction continued long after his death in 1547. The widowed Queen Catherine de' Medici consulted her astrologers in an observatory built in the central lantern.

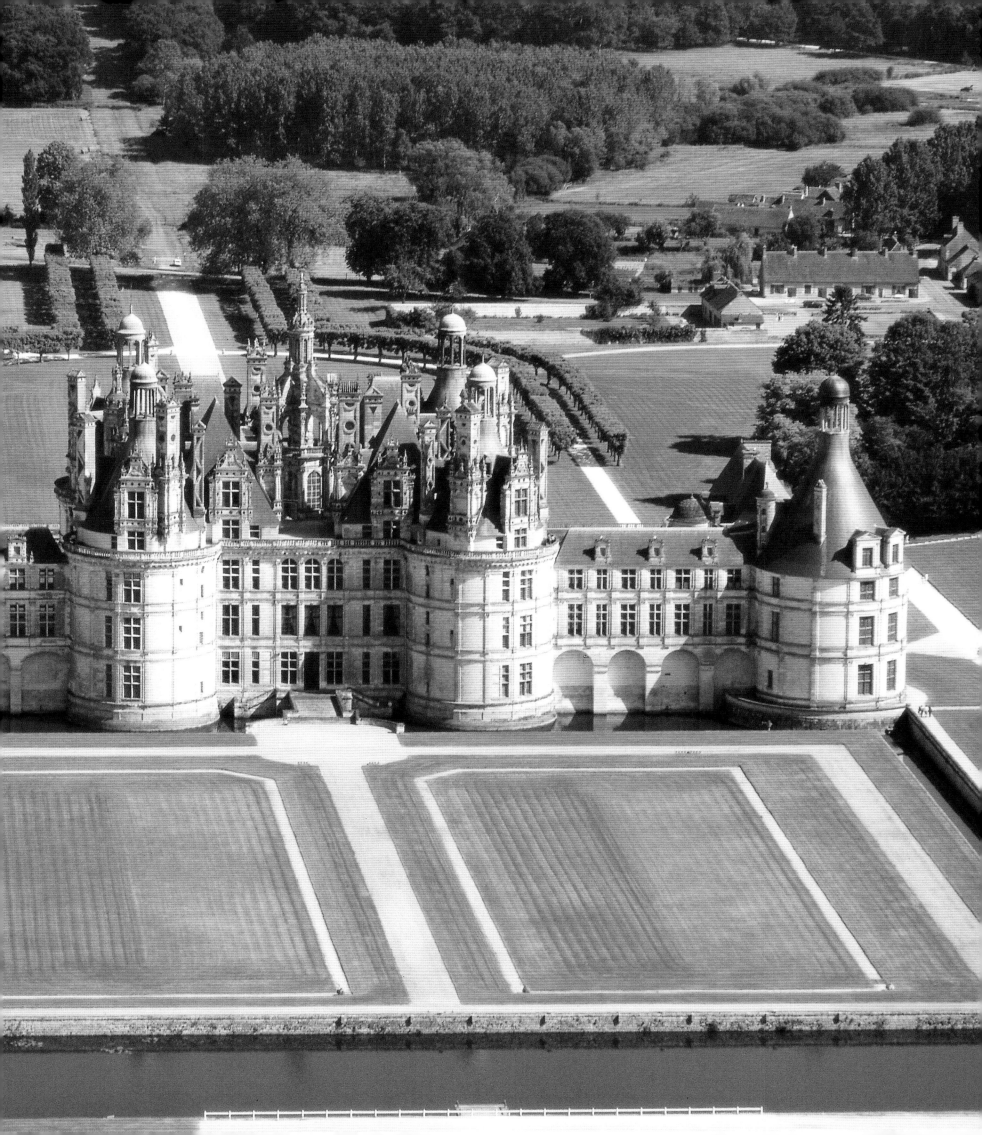

Chateau de Blois, France

The royal chateau of Blois makes an intriguing guide to the development of French palace architecture from Gothic to Renaissance. In 1635–8 the Orléans wing was added by the greatest architect of seventeenth-century France, François Mansart (1598–1666). This wing has a sense of lucid classicism, of restraint and pure design, contrasting with the exuberance of the earlier parts. It was Mansart, too, who established the unmistakable look of the French chateau, with its pitched roof and truncated-pyramidal pavilions.

Fontainebleau

Blois can hardly be called a palace, but Fontainebleau, François I's "second Rome" near Paris, undoubtedly is. François I (reigned 1515–47) built the main courtyard, the long gallery, and the Porte Dorée (Golden Gateway) and laid out the long approach avenue in the true Renaissance style. A team of Italian artists, led by Francesco Primaticcio (1504–70) and Rosso Fiorentino (1494–1540), gave it a

The Palace of Fontainebleau, France

The buildings of 1528–40 have been called "the most complete early Renaissance ensemble in France." The architect was Gilles le Breton (died 1553). Right: The throne room, Fontainebleau, refurbished by Napoleon Bonaparte (emperor 1804–15).

magnificent interior of fresco, carved wood, stucco, marble panels, and sculpture. A French innovation, first found at Fontainebleau, was a long gallery. This feature, presumably intended for parading up and down in an indoor form of the Italian *passeggiata*, and richly decorated with stucco and with fine murals by Fiorentino and Primaticcio, was to become one of the standard elements without which no monarch felt a palace to be complete.

The Louvre

In 1541, the French architect Pierre Lescot (*c.*1515–78) began work on the Square Court of the Louvre Palace in Paris. This established the French Renaissance style, with its strong, rhythmic, and emphatic form that was able to contain a great deal of decoration without being overwhelmed. One feature that French architects, working in a more northerly climate, had to take into account was the presence of chimney stacks, and Chambord and Lescot's Louvre show how these, in different ways, were integrated into the design — in the one as lofty turrets; in the other as sculptural punctuation marks of the roof-line.

Palace of the Louvre, Paris, France

Above: One of the central pavilions in the Cour du Carousel (seventeenth century). Earlier architects would have balked at the use of double columns purely for decoration, serving no constructional purpose, but in the baroque era, decoration was what mattered.

Right: Built as a royal palace, the Louvre, splendidly floodlit here, is now a palace of art and culture.

Versailles

Few palaces remained unchanged. Evolving notions of taste, the style of court life, and the desire for comfort all ensured that the buildings would be worked over or extended. Each generation of royal or princely owners wanted to make its own mark, unless prevented by war or lack of cash. Palaces such as Windsor (see page 53) reveal some very different styles over 900 years of English architecture. Versailles, however, in its hundred years of building, shows an almost organic development from the style of one generation to the next. But essentially it is a tremendous achievement of the French baroque, using every device of Renaissance architecture and design to suggest grandeur and opulence, but within the restraints of elegance and order.

In 1624 Louis XIII of France (reigned 1610–43) built a small hunting lodge on the knoll of Versailles, near Paris. It was a marshy, bushy, insalubrious region, but Louis liked his hunting lodge and gradually improved and enlarged it into a handsome chateau. Under the 72-year reign of his son, Louis XIV (reigned 1643–1715), it was to become the definitive palace. Versailles, begun in 1669, was the wonder of Europe.

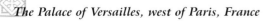 *The Palace of Versailles, west of Paris, France*

The central block, constructed by Le Vau in 1668–70.

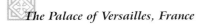

The Palace of Versailles, France

Above: The opera house of Louis XV.

Right: The Hall of Mirrors, decorated by Le Brun (1678–84).

It was the biggest palace, the grandest, the most superbly decorated, the most brilliantly landscaped. At one and the same time it set the standard and guaranteed that nothing should outdo it. No other kingdom had the combination of financial resources, artistic talent, and inflexible autocratic will to create something on this scale. Even as Louis XIV's palace was going up, it was clear that it would set the pattern. It was not original in concept, but it gathered together all the strands of Renaissance and post-Renaissance palace-building and garden design and combined them into an awesome unity. Even the stables are magnificent.

Versailles is the creation of many thousands of laborers and craftsmen, but three men chiefly directed its form: André Le Nôtre (1613–1700), who designed the park, Louis Le Vau (1612–70), who built the terraces, and Jules Hardouin-Mansart (1646–1708), who in the 30 years between 1678 and 1708 gave the palace its present form. Le Nôtre's vision transformed the wastelands into a grandly landscaped formal park, with the mile-long Grand Canal and an

ÉTABLISSEMENT
DE L'HOSTEL ROYAL
DES INVALIDES
1674.

The Palace of Versailles, France

Left: A detail from the ceiling of the Hall of Mirrors.

Right: The bedroom of Louis XIV. The bust of the

king is by Antoine Coysevox (1640–1720).

elaborate pattern of lawns, parterres, trees, topiary hedges, lakes, fountains (a thousand of them), and innumerable sculptures, including the chariot of the sun rising from the water, one of the omnipresent symbols of the Sun King, who was the living focus of the entire scheme. Le Vau retained Louis XIII's chateau as the central block, framing the Cour de Marbre (Marble Courtyard). Mansart, a great-nephew of the great French architect François Mansart, added the garden front, the Hall of Mirrors (1678–84), with its 17 huge mirrors, on what had been an outside terrace, the north and south wings, and the lofty chapel, oddly Gothic with its flying buttresses. In the gardens he constructed the Grand Trianon, a large, ornate garden house to which the king could retreat.

Throughout the eighteenth century, the additions continued. The Opera House was built by Jean-Ange (or Jacques-Ange) Gabriel (1698–1742) in the reign of Louis XV (1715–74). He also built the Petit Trianon between 1762 and 1770. The last building, the Hameau, a mock-rustic hamlet where Queen Marie Antoinette dressed as a dairymaid, was completed only three years before the French Revolution, when the splendors of Versailles were ransacked by the long-exploited citizens, and King Louis XVI was dragged to prison and execution.

Life in the palace was intended to be as ceremonious and stately as the building itself. Part of the reason for the vastness of the place was to accommodate the horde of great nobles who participated in the rituals

of the king's levée, assisting the monarch with his shirt or his stockings, and joining in the hunts, entertainments, and feasts. In his youth Louis XIV had lived through rebellion by the nobles, and he successfully neutralized their power by turning them into courtiers. The court moved from the Louvre in 1682, and later the entire machinery of government was transferred to Versailles. Some 1000 courtiers and 4000 servants lived there. Life was very public, with one great room opening on to the next. The function was display, not utility. Where a Roman emperor would have incorporated a great baths complex, the Sun King, 1700 years later, had none. His grandees, when taken short, had to relieve themselves on the stairs. But these were the expectations of the age.

SPAIN

The Escorial

In Spain, a country with a unique architectural heritage — Moorish-Visigothic-High Gothic — the Renaissance took shape with one of the most remarkable palaces in history. Philip II of Spain (reigned 1556–98) commissioned a vast edifice to be built thirty miles (48 kilometers) from his capital; this was the Escorial (constructed 1563–1584), in part a mausoleum for his father, Charles V. As a tribute to imperial wealth, extravagant piety, and the totalitarian spirit, it has never been rivaled. The architect, Juan Bautista de Toledo (d.1567), had worked with Michelangelo in Rome, and he brought to Spain all the monumentality of the great Italian. Perhaps it was Philip himself who froze out the humanity.

The Escorial incorporates a vast church, a monastery, and a seminary as well as a palace proper. Its austerity is enhanced by the granite of which it is constructed, and the classical orders, more apparent in the horizontal than in the vertical plane, are subdued in the monotonous regularity of the mass. Philip II had a tiny room, abutting the church and looking down toward the high altar. It was in this room that he died. The Escorial had been completed by Toledo's assistant, Juan de Herrera (c.1530–97), who went on to perpetuate the same somewhat cheerless style in other palaces and public buildings.

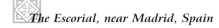

The Escorial, near Madrid, Spain

Right: The fresco in the vault of the grand staircase, by Giordano Luca (1632–1705), showing the Triumph of the Habsburgs.

Below: The colossal scale of the Escorial is well conveyed in this aerial view, which also shows how the church is integrated into the palace plan.

BRITAIN

Henry VIII of England (reigned 1509–47) owned more houses than any English monarch before or since — over sixty. There were several reasons for this, in addition to Henry's well-developed ego. His court, numbering some 1500 people, had all to be accommodated in the larger palaces. They could not stay in any one place too long because of the inadequate feeding and sanitary arrangements. Here, as in France, the palaces had to be fumigated and scrubbed out after a few months' occupancy. The building of a country palace, such as the now-vanished Nonsuch, near Epsom in Surrey, built in 1538 and demolished in the 1680s, was intended to provide the king with a house where he could be alone, relatively speaking, with perhaps only a couple of hundred courtiers and retainers. (Nonsuch was probably modeled on Chambord.) Uniquely among

European countries, England did not employ Italian architects, although English architects undoubtedly traveled to the continent and studied the manuals closely.

Hampton Court

Despite his many dwellings, Henry and his daughter Elizabeth I (reigned 1558–1603) also expected to be entertained by their more prominent subjects. This was one of the reasons for the scale of Cardinal Wolsey's Hampton Court, a palace that he sensibly presented to the king in 1529 before the king simply took it for himself. Hampton Court remained a royal palace. In 1689, King William III commissioned Sir Christopher Wren (1632–1723), the architect of St. Paul's Cathedral, to rebuild it, but the project stopped with the death of William's co-ruler, Mary, in 1694, and the palace remains part-Tudor, part-English baroque.

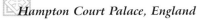

Hampton Court Palace, England

Cardinal Wolsey presented his palace to Henry VIII.

The Tudor part is by the river. Although the state apartments of Henry VIII are now lost, the great hall survives, with its roof of hammer-beam trusses. The cardinal's private rooms are also still to be seen, showing an interesting blend of native motifs, such as linenfold paneling, and Renaissance-influenced painting and decoration. The Tudor kitchens remain, the brick halls lit from high windows, as does the elaborate Tudor chapel, with its Gothic false vault made of wood and plaster and its trumpeting English putti. Wren's façade faces away from the river into a formal garden. By this time, Versailles was underway and its influence on palace architecture was already supreme. It has even been suggested that the renewal of Hampton Court was stopped because the English monarch realized that he could not afford to compete with Louis XIV. Wren's palace is nevertheless very English in its detail, its use of brickwork (three different sorts of brick), and even in its less than megalomaniac scale. It manages to achieve an intimate, almost domestic feeling that is not at all evoked by Versailles.

Windsor Castle

A little further up the Thames, accessible from Hampton Court by the royal barge, was another favorite royal residence, Windsor Castle. Properly speaking, Windsor is a castle, with massive fortified walls, but from the twelfth century, kings had used its spacious site to build a residence within the walls. Edward III (reigned 1327–77) had a palace there in the fourteenth century; its vaults now support St. George's Hall. St. George's Chapel was begun in 1472 and finished in 1538.

Henry VIII played tennis at Windsor. The gatehouse was added in his time, but the state apartments as they are today were built under Charles II (reigned 1660–85) in the seventeenth century and George IV (reigned 1820–30) in the nineteenth century. Charles commissioned the North Terrace, the rather austere classical lines of which contained some of the finest wood-carving in England, the work of Grinling Gibbons (1648–1721)

Windsor Castle, England

Above: The magnificent Crimson Drawing Room, part of the State Apartments at Windsor.

Right: The castle's forbidding walls belie the comfort and luxury within.

and Philipps. Twenty ceilings, of which three remain, were painted by the Italian Antonio Verrio (c.1639–1707). Charles, who had seen Versailles, began the great avenue that stretches for 3 miles (5 kilometers) to the south. In 1824 a major restoration and rebuilding was undertaken by George IV, with Sir Jeffry Wyatville (1766–1840) as his architect. The Waterloo Chamber and the Grand Corridor were added. In 1995 Windsor Castle was partly devastated by fire. Restoration was completed in 1997.

CHAPTER FIVE

PALACES OF

Russia and the

NORDIC LANDS

RUSSIA

Moscow

Awooden-walled stockade protected the settlement of Moscow in 1147. From here in 1380 the prince of Moscow, Dmitri Ivanovich, rode out to defeat the Golden Horde at Kulikovo. His great grandson, Ivan III, the Great (reigned 1440–1505), married the Byzantine princess Zoë Palaeologus in 1472. In that year an earthquake destroyed much of the capital, and the Italian architect-engineer Ridolfo Aristotele Fioravanti (*c.*1415–86) was brought to superintend the rebuilding. By this time the Kremlin, at the heart of the city, was the center of temporal and spiritual government, an astounding assemblage of four cathedrals, royal palaces, imperial workshops, and treasuries. At its center the Red Square, a name that long predates Communist rule, formed a great open space around which fantastic cupola-topped buildings arose. In the exact center of the Kremlin stands the Bell Tower of Ivan the Great, 270 feet (82 meters) high and hung with 33 bells, built in 1600 by Tsar Boris Godunov.

This most Russian of enclaves owes an enormous amount to Fioravanti and his Italian successors, Antonio Solario (*c.*1450–93) and Ruffo, who learned how to employ characteristic Russian themes. They built the Palace of Facets (1487–1491), its prismatic stone walls contemporaneous with those of the Palazzo dei Diamanti in Ferrara. Its great feature is the throne room with its single pillar supporting the vault.

Adjacent to it is the so-called Garret Palace (Teremnoi Dvorets). Begun in 1508 and destroyed seven times in the turbulent

The Kremlin, Moscow, Russia

This view from beyond the walls and over the Moscow River shows the lofty Bell Tower built by Boris Godunov and gives a sense of the complexity and extent of the palace site.

history of Russia, it was finally rebuilt in 1613–76 in the form that still remains. These were the private apartments of the tsars, richly decorated with frescoes and painted leather. The walls and ceiling of the golden room are lined in leather, decorated with religious themes and gilded arabesques. Gold and silver inlays decorate the ceiling arches. The window panes of tinted mica give the room its pink aura.

The tsar's bedroom opened directly into the throne room. In each chamber, a massive tiled stove was integrated into the decorative scheme. In the security of the palace demesne

and under the eye of the tsar, immigrant and Russian artificers worked in the Oruzhemaya Palata, the Armorers' Chamber, a great workshop for both weaponry and for art. The present building, dating from the first half of the nineteenth century, holds a stupendous collection of weapons, robes, thrones, carriages, silver plate, and ceramics.

In the 1830s, Nicholas I (reigned 1825–55) had most of the old Kremlin palace buildings flattened to make room for the new Kremlin Grand Palace, completed in

1849. In contrast to the previous imperial splendor, the Grand Kremlin Palace became the meeting-place of the Supreme Soviet, which met in a studiedly plain edifice built on the site of two former chapels.

The Kremlin, one of the world's great treasure houses, still harbors the fabulous objects accumulated by the tsars, both works of Russian art and gifts from foreign monarchs. Its holdings include the Cap of Monomakh, jeweled symbol of Russian kingship, the crown of Kazan, which

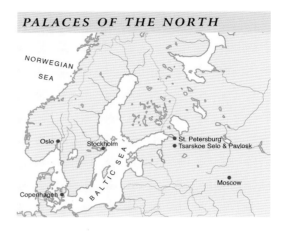

PALACES OF THE NORTH

Peter the Great brought European architecture to Russia in 1705 and began the imperial Russian taste for palace-building. In the Nordic countries, too, the Age of Reason saw the influence of sophisticated new European styles.

replicates the cupola of St. Basil's Cathedral, the Ivory Throne (fifteenth century), the Diamond Throne of Alexis Mikhaylovich (reigned 1645–76), the state coach sent by Elizabeth I of England to Boris Godunov, the wedding gown of Catherine II, the Great (reigned 1762–96), and the renowned Fabergé eggs of Alexander III (reigned 1881–94).

St. Petersburg

In 1705, Peter the Great (reigned 1682–1725) founded St. Petersburg. He built a relatively modest palace in the Dutch style on the Winter Dike, linking the Moika River to the wide Neva, which was replaced by a

The Winter Palace, St. Petersburg, Russia

The palace's uninhibited ormolu interior is in the typically vigorous Russian Imperial style.

The Winter Palace, St. Petersburg, Russia

The much-restored front seen from across a suitably wintry Palace Square.

palace on the Neva itself. This, in turn, was enlarged, but in 1753 the Italian architect Bartolomeo Rastrelli (1700–71) persuaded the Empress Elizabeth to start afresh. From Rastrelli's designs come the great palace that stands today. It was completed by 1759, although alterations, as ever in palaces, went on. A fire in 1837 caused major damage, as did the siege endured by the city in the Second World War. Each time, the exterior was restored, although after 1837 the interior was substantially altered.

The palace is a long rectangle, its two main fronts — to the river and the palace square — open to view. Over 656 feet (200 meters) long and 98 feet (30 meters) high, it is a monumental structure, built to occupy a monumental setting. Rastrelli's interior designs were gradually changed by later architects and in the aftermath of the fire of 1837. In 1826 Karl Ivanovich Rossi (1775–1849) designed the 1812 Gallery to commemorate the heroes of the Napoleonic War. Of the 1500 rooms of the palace, the state rooms remain a reasonably faithful replica of the originals, although the truly original remaining part is the majestic grand staircase. The Empress Catherine had the Hermitage designed by a French architect, Jean-Baptiste-Michel Vallin de la Mothe (1729–1800). It was her private retreat and her place for putting aside the distance lent by her imperial status, when entertaining such friends as the philosopher Denis Diderot. Now the annex has taken over the identity of the whole, and the Winter Palace is the Hermitage Museum.

Tsarskoe Selo

The name of Catherine is more closely associated with Tsarskoe Selo (Tsar's Village), near St. Petersburg. Her predecessor, Elizabeth, had a taste for the extravagant and for her, in 1749–56, Rastrelli had built a lusciously rococo palace with a distinctively Russian flavor. It is vast — 1000 feet (305 meters) long — and in its original form blazed white and gold in the sunlight. It was too much for Catherine the Great, who toned down the gilding to bronze.

Less than ten years after the palace was finished, Catherine had the east wing completely altered by her favorite architect, the exiled Jacobite Scot Charles Cameron (*c.*1743–1812). Catherine's private rooms include the Chinese salon, the Salon de Lyon, a French drawing room whose wall-coverings were striped yellow silk, the silver room, and the blue room (nicknamed "the snuffbox" and still with its original furniture). Cameron also designed the colonnade and the agate pavilion, with its beautiful medallions and bas-reliefs by the French sculptor Jean-Dominique Rachette. In the park, amid pools and woods, stand exquisite lesser buildings, including the Chinese Summerhouse.

Tsarskoe Selo, Russia

Tsarskoe Selo suffered greatly during the Second World War, and its glories, although painstakingly restored, have a slightly muted and melancholy air.

Palace of Petrodvorets, near St. Petersburg

Above: Also known as Peterhof, this is another of Rastrelli's masterpieces. The building and gardens have been restored since the Second World War.

The Pavlovsk Palace, near Tsarskoe Selo

Left: The palace was built in the early 1780s by Charles Cameron for the son of Catherine the Great, although the curving wings, an interior from one of which is seen here, were added by Vincenzo Brenna (1745–1820).

SCANDINAVIA

From the imperial splendors and grandiose eccentricities of Imperial Russia to the Scandinavian palaces is a relatively short journey in space but a long one in spirit. Three of the Scandinavian countries remain monarchies — unobtrusive, relatively informal constitutional monarchies, with little in the way of pomp and ceremony. But the royal palaces date from an earlier era, when the Scandinavian monarchs were sovereigns and expected to show it.

Amalienborg

Perhaps the most unusual of these royal palaces is Amalienborg, in the Danish capital, Copenhagen. It is in fact four separate palaces, set on the eight sides of the spacious Amalienborg Plads (the name commemorates a castle once built there). The present Queen of Denmark, a highly respected figure, lives in the palace to the right of the entrance to the Plads, one of the finest city piazzas in Europe, very close to the quays. The setting of such grandeur in a humdrum townscape is part of its charm. Two of the palaces are in use as homes, while the others are used for state events and also house a museum of royal treasures.

Built by the pleasure-loving Frederick V of Denmark (reigned 1746–66), they were not originally intended for royal use, but as houses for the nobility. The kings lived in the palace of Christiansborg but moved to Amalienborg when the former house was destroyed by fire in 1794. Designed by Niels Eigtved and the German architect Marcus Tuscher, the buildings began to go up in 1750. The four original owners were given a free hand with the interiors.

The first owner of the royal palace was Adam Gottlob Moltke, councilor to the king. He made it a gem of northern European rococo, commissioning the splendid Riddersalen, or Knights' Hall, by François de Cuvilliés (1695–1768). It has white paneled walls, decorated with carved and gilt ornamentation, and a stucco ceiling. The pictures above the two fireplaces and doors are by François Boucher (1703–70). Moltke moved in 1754, but work continued on the dining hall. The classicism of this fine pillared room shows how late in the rococo period the palace comes; the reaction towards a new classicism was already beginning.

Stockholm

Grandest of the Nordic palaces is that of Stockholm. During the sixteenth and seventeenth centuries, Sweden had become a major power in northern Europe. The brilliant campaigns of Gustavus Adolphus at the head of his army in the Thirty Years' War (1618–48) were still well remembered, and it was felt that the king of Sweden, Charles XI (reigned 1660–97), merited a palace the world would admire.

The Palace of Drottningholm, Sweden

The Swedish royal family's country palace and main home. The name means "queen's island," and the central block was built in 1662 by Nicodemus Tessin the Elder (1615–81) for Queen Eleonora. The palace grounds hold a charming baroque theater.

The building that resulted is a strong tribute to absolute monarchy. Vast in size, monumental in position and overall design, it was intended to dominate the city from its island site. Luckily for its original architect, Nicodemus Tessin the Younger (1654–1728), the previous palace was destroyed by fire just at the time he was commissioned to make alterations to it. He was able to make a new start. He had been deeply impressed by a visit to Versailles in 1687, where he had admired not just the general design but the detail and the workmanship of French craftsmen.

Tessin's palace shows also his admiration for the façades of late-Renaissance Italy in its severity of manner. This was to have been alleviated by statues rising above the balustrade, but lack of money meant these were never commissioned. By 1710 the structure was complete, and some interior work had been done, when money ran out. Tessin had to bide his time until 1728 to resume again but died that same year.

The forbidding aspect of the outside is forgotten once the interior is seen. Here Tessin's passion for French taste, passed on to his son Carl Gustav Tessin (1695–1770), who completed the work with the Paris-taught Carl Horleman, was given full reign. As Stockholm's palace did not pass through the vicissitudes of Versailles and other French palaces, its decoration and furnishings act as a time-capsule for the splendor of pre-Revolutionary France. Among the finest rooms are the Charles XI Gallery, inspired by the Hall of Mirrors at Versailles, and the White Sea Gallery with its *trompe l'oeil* paintings done in the 1730s by Domenico Francia. The chapel, not French in inspiration but following the Italian baroque of Gian Lorenzo Bernini (1598–1680), has superb French works including J.-P. Bouchardon's pulpit and J.-F. Cousinet's beautiful silver font. Other fine

work by Bouchardon includes the bronze lanterns on the monumental west staircase. Many French artists and craftsmen were invited to Sweden. Some spent so much time there that they were almost forgotten in their native country. The architects also bought in tapestries by Boucher, Savonnerie carpets, gilt candelabra, dinner services, mirrors, and many other fine furnishings.

It was 1754 when the royal family actually took occupancy of the palace. By now the finishing touches were being done by yet another French-trained Swede, Jean Eric Rehn. But things in Paris had moved on since Tessin's visit in the previous century, and Rehn's contribution is a steelier, colder, though elegant Louis XVI style.

Royal Palace, Oslo, Norway

The Royal Palace in Oslo, commandingly placed on the hill, with a clear vista from Karl Johans Gate, is the most finely sited. Oddly enough, there was no king of independent Norway when it was commissioned in 1818. The crown of Norway for centuries had been united with that of, first Denmark, and then Sweden. The king who commissioned it was Karl XIV Johan (reigned 1818–44), better known to history as Napoleon's Marshal Bernadotte. It was 1906 before it became the home of King Haakon of again-independent Norway.

The palace was designed on strict classical lines by H.D.F. Linstow, whose original conception was on the grand scale. It envisaged an H-shaped, three-storied central block, with wings coming forward at right angles. But the final building, largely for cost reasons, is simpler, although still stately. A lofty portico of Ionic columns on top of an arched base is flanked by a long façade, with end pavilions defined by a slight projection. Inside are some imposing rooms, including two ballrooms. Not as pretty as Amalienborg, not as grand as Stockholm, it manages to exude a fitting sense of unostentatious Norwegian-ness.

CHAPTER SIX

THE CROWNED HEADS OF EUROPE:

Royal PALACES

During the second millennium, as the major kingdoms of Europe gradually formed, other lesser kingdoms and principalities rose, fell, and sometimes rose again. Wars between the greater powers quenched some small states and gave birth to others. The fortunes of their rulers varied, too. While monarchy remained strong in western Europe, the twentieth century saw its disappearance in central and eastern Europe.

Buckingham Palace, London, England

The imposing modern (1913) front of Buckingham Palace, seen from St James's Park.

BRITAIN

London has three royal palaces that remain royal residences, St James's, Kensington, and Buckingham. St James's Palace dates back to the days of Henry VIII, although little remains from that period except the fine Tudor gateway, built around 1535. It is the London home of Prince Charles. Kensington Palace, originally a country house of the Earl of Nottingham, was bought by William III, who wanted a house nearer than Hampton Court to the center of government at Whitehall. It was turned into a palace by Sir Christopher Wren (1632–1723) and further extended by William Kent (1684–1748), and was the preferred royal residence until the reign of George III. Until her death in 1997, it was the home of Diana, Princess of Wales.

Buckingham Palace, in the center of London, was originally built in the early eighteenth century as the London house of the dukes of Buckingham. As Buckingham House, it was bought in 1762 by George III (reigned 1760–1820), who made it his London residence. Compared to his fellow-monarchs' palaces, it was a rather modest establishment. Its transformation happened by degrees, beginning with the reign of George IV (1820–30). His architect John Nash (1752–1835) enlarged the building, giving it a main façade looking on to the gardens, flanked by two Ionic-columned orangery pavilions. The garden front, partly visible from the high-rise buildings to the west, is wide and low, handsomely built of warm-coloured Bath stone, with the effect of a charming country house. The rear was open, with two wings stretching toward the Mall. London's Marble Arch, now at the upper end of Park Lane, originally stood in the center between the ends of the wings. Nash's building was not finished by the time Queen Victoria came to the throne in 1837, and further additions soon began. The two wings were joined, making the building quadrangular, and in 1855 the south side

was further enlarged by the construction of the ballroom and the State Supper Room. The aim was to have a palace in the capital to match the status of a Queen-Empress, but she did not care for London, and much preferred Windsor. It was not until the twentieth century that Buckingham Palace really became the focus of state pageantry. The present dignified front, facing down the Mall, was built in 1913, during the reign of George V. The old front then became the rear and Nash's fine setting for the palace at last came into its own.

NETHERLANDS

The kingdom of the Netherlands, which came into being in 1815, was centered on the ancient countship of Holland. The Dutch Parliament now meets in what was the counts' palace in The Hague. The first king, William I (reigned 1815–40), acquired three palaces, but also took over the Huis

ten Bosch (House in the Wood), near The Hague, as a summer palace. Built in 1645 for Prince Frederick Henry by a Dutch architect, Pieter Post (1608–69), it shows a happy blend of Dutch tradition and Palladian style. It was enlarged in the 1730s by the French baroque architect Daniel Marot (1661–1752), who added the wings without destroying the unity of the building.

Inside, the most impressive room is the Oranjesaal, dating from the original building, a tribute to Frederick Henry, who died in 1647, with paintings by Jacob Jordaens (1593–1678), Gerrit van Honthorst (1590–1656), and other Dutch masters decorating its walls. The wealth gained by Holland from the East Indies is indicated in the decoration and furnishing of the Chinese and Japanese rooms dating from the late eighteenth century. Under the

Huis ten Bosch, Netherlands

The lofty Oranjesaal, whose decorated walls merge into the arched ceiling.

German Occupation in the Second World War, the palace was to have been demolished; happily it survives, and now the central block is used for state receptions, the left wing as a royal residence, and the right wing for guests.

BELGIUM

In 1830, the kingdom of the Belgians was formed from the southern part of the Netherlands, with Brussels as its capital.

Kensington Palace, London, England

Lived in by various members of the British royal family at different times, it was referred to by Edward VII as "the aunt-heap." Most recently it was the home of Diana, Princess of Wales.

THE CROWNED HEADS OF EUROPE: ROYAL PALACES LARGE AND SMALL

Until the late eighteenth century, much of eastern Europe and the Balkans was controlled by the Ottoman Empire, based in Turkey. With the decline of the Ottomans in the East and the defeat of Napoleon in the West, Europe saw the revival of many small, independent kingdoms and dukedoms – the Ruritania of palaces, crown princes, royal weddings, and international high society beloved of Hollywood. The nineteenth century was the heyday of European monarchies, few of which survived the wars and revolutions of the twentieth.

Neuschwanstein Castle, Bavaria, Germany

This fantasy castle-palace is the best known of Ludwig II's buildings.

Brussels has two palaces, the Royal Palace in the center, which is used as an office, and Laeken Palace in the suburb of Tervueren. Laeken was built in 1782–4, and rebuilt in 1890 after a fire. It employs the elements of palace architecture — imposing pillared portico, dome, balustrades, cornices, and so forth — in a rather uninspired way. It is very much a private residence, although its park has been open to the public for many years.

It has famous hothouses, a legacy of Leopold II (reigned 1865–1909), who ruled the vast Belgian Congo as though it were his personal estate.

BAVARIA

King Ludwig II of Bavaria was eventually certified as mad, but in his 22-year reign (1864–86) he commissioned a succession of buildings that still enchant visitors. His preference was for castles, where his admiration for the composer Richard Wagner is very evident, but at Linderhof in the German Alps he built a country palace in

Linderhof, Bavaria, Germany

This miniature Versailles (built 1874–9) is King Ludwig II's tribute to the Sun King.

the style and spirit of Louis XIV — with a touch of Grimm's fairy tales added. Designed by the royal architect, Georg Dollmann (1830–1895), and built in 1874–9, it totally transformed an old hunting lodge and remains the only one of Ludwig's schemes to be completed.

Its front, seen across a swan-inhabited pool and set on a terrace reached by a double staircase, shows a strong, sober, rusticated ground floor with triple entrance arches, and above it a tall piano nobile, more decorative, with a bronze-railed balcony, lushly carved capitals, a giant central niche holding a statue of Victory, and smaller statues in the lateral niches. Rising above is a riotous composition of statuary and deeply carved coat of arms, the whole crowned by a statue of Atlas holding the world a trifle precariously on one shoulder.

Despite their splendor, Ludwig's palaces were private places, built purely for his own pleasure. Linderhof's interior is a window into his imagination — here he could be Louis rather than Ludwig. His gilt and velvet bed,

Herrenchiemsee, Bavaria, Germany

Right: In 1878, on an island in the Chiemsee lake, Ludwig now began a full-size replica of Versailles, but only the central section was built. Still the largest of Ludwig's palaces, it boasts a splendid Hall of Mirrors(below).

with its swags of gold, has a balustrade to separate the favored from the "ordinary" courtiers. The dining room has a table that can be let down from above, already laid, so that the king, like some prince in an enchanter's palace, could dine without seeing another living soul. The beautiful park of Linderhof, with its ornamental lake, 100-foot (30-meter)-high fountain, and cast-iron Moorish kiosk, also has a highly theatrical

grotto whose inspiration seems to owe more to Wagner's operas than to the Sun King. Ludwig went on to build a still grander French baroque palace at Herrenchiemsee, on a lake island, but Linderhof remained his favorite.

ITALY

The Quirinal

In 1870, Italy ceased to be a network of kingdoms and principalities and became a unified kingdom "by the grace of God and the will of the nation" under Victor Emmanuel II of Savoy (reigned 1861–78). The temporal domain of the papacy was reduced to the Vatican City, and the new king took over the papal palace, the Quirinal,

although, because the pope refused to hand over the keys, it had to be burgled. On the relatively airy site of the Quirinal Hill, it was originally built from 1547 as a summer palace, but Clement VIII made it his permanent residence. Some of the greatest artists of the Renaissance contributed to it, including Carlo Maderno (1556–1629), who worked on the front, and Gian Lorenzo Bernini (1598–1680), who designed the main entrance.

The royal, now presidential, apartments are in the *palazzetto* (little palace) at the end of the long wing overlooking the Via Quirinale. The palace chapel, with frescoes

by Michelangelo, used to be the scene of papal elections. The Quirinal has a hall of mirrors with fine Venetian glass chandeliers and another almost obligatory feature of the European palace in the eighteenth century, a chinoiserie drawing room.

Turin

Set almost informally on a street in close-packed Rome, the Quirinal is not the most imposingly sited of Italian palaces. Nor is the Royal Palace of Turin, where the dukes of Savoy had ruled before they became kings of Italy. It has a sober, undemonstrative front (begun 1646) that gives no indication of the exuberance within.

Monaco

Left and right: At the Mediterranean end of Europe, the tiny principality of Monaco has been ruled by the Grimaldi family since the thirteenth century. Honoré II transformed the medieval castle into a palace in the early seventeenth century, by commissioning Italian architects and artists to extend new apartments and arcaded galleries round the old building. Honoré II was a keen patron of art, and among his 700 or so acquisitions were a number of Titian portraits. His grandson, Louis I, was responsible for the great pedimented doorway and the staircase modeled on that of Fontainebleau in France. The French Revolution temporarily dislodged the Grimaldis, and the palace was used as a barracks and then a poor-house. Aided by the growing wealth of Monaco as a resort and casino town, the restored dynasty also restored the palace, and it is now home to a splendid collection of fine art, silverware, mementos of the Bonapartes, and Prince Rainier III's Stamp Museum.

The baroque style as seen in Italy and the other Latin countries was far less restrained than in northern Europe, and, while it often gets lost in a welter of overdone detail, in the hands of a great artist it could create remarkable effects.

The royal palace of Turin has its own access to the cathedral, home of Turin's most venerated relic, the Holy Shroud. Guarino Guarini (1624–83) completed the building, with its brilliantly conceived and executed openwork dome. The east wing, now the

imposing Armory, was completed at the same time. In the eighteenth century the palace was remodeled by Filippo Juvarra or Juvara (1678–1736), who designed the scissor staircase and the superb Chinese room, with its delicate scrollwork, mirrors, and lacquer panels. The glittering, incredibly detailed inlay work of Pietro Piffetti gives a touch of enchantment to the Maria Theresa room and the tiny royal chapel. The sumptuous tradition extends, with a touch more pomp and less elegance, into the nineteenth-century throne room and ballroom. These and the alcove room, the work of Pelagio Palagi (1775–1860), show the magnificence of gilding taken to its ultimate effect, and possibly beyond. But the splendor is undeniable.

Stupinigi

Early in the eighteenth century, the Savoys set about creating a country palace outside Turin at Stupinigi, where they already had a modest hunting box. Filippo Juvarra, who had trained as a theatrical designer, designed a most imposing building, whose tall central oval, its dome surmounted by a gilded stag, had four radiating wings in the form of a St. Andrew's cross, as well as two long, obliquely angled lateral wings, which end in pavilions. The curves and angles form an interesting comparison to Versailles. Despite its great size it remains a country house dedicated to the pleasures of the chase — hunting motifs are everywhere in the interior — rather than a seat of absolute power.

Palace at Caserta, Italy

Under King Ferdinand II (1810–59), in this brooding palace "linen was hung up to dry in marble halls; the children romped with the servants and played crude practical jokes on their tutors and governesses; the Queen sat over her sewing near the cradle of her latest infant; while the King rocked another baby in his arms and distributed lollipops."

Caserta

Perhaps the most determined effort to reproduce both the atmosphere and the combined pleasure/administrative role of Versailles was that of the Bourbon Charles III, who became king of Naples in 1734 at the age of 18 and ruled there until he departed to become king of Spain in 1759. An enthusiastic palace builder, he was not content with the old royal palace in the city, or his new palaces of Capodimonte and Portici. He commissioned a palace at Caserta to be both a residence and a center of government.

Charles's architect, Luca (Luigi) Vanvitelli (1700–73), designed the entire colossal scheme inside a year, and the foundation stone was laid in 1752. Conscript and slave labor was used in the task of hauling stone and laying out the gardens. Vanvitelli had Versailles as a model, but he took advantage of the lie of the land to create the cascade, with its extraordinarily lifelike statues of Diana, Actaeon, nymphs, and dogs. A perfectly straight 16-mile (26-kilometer) avenue, was intended to link it to Naples, with a 2-mile (3-kilometer) continuation through the great park at the rear.

Vanvitelli had planned corner towers and a central dome, but these were never built and the great front is a rigidly horizontal and austere wall from which the more than one hundred windows seem to gaze unblinkingly. Once inside the entrance arch, however, a huge vestibule cuts through the whole width and reveals the dramatic perspective of a distant cataract. Below the point at which the dome would have been, a great octagonal opening gives vistas into the four inner courts.

Caserta, never completed internally, is a building of prospects and vistas, like some vast artificial cave, overwhelming but fascinating. The rooms on the south front, to the right of the main entrance, were the first to be inhabited. Work went on under Charles III's increasingly eccentric successors, and the apartments with their Louis XV and XVI decoration and furnishing show how French taste dominated Europe from Stockholm to Naples. But with its proximity to Pompeii, Caserta also often shows a classical touch, with Roman-style wall-paintings, and the theater (1796) uses green marble columns removed from the nearby temple of Serapis. On the left of the entrance, the Appartamento Nuovo shows the continuing history of Naples under Napoleon's marshal Joachim Murat.

THE BALKANS
Athens

The stormy history of the Balkan states, as they fought themselves free of the Ottoman Empire in the nineteenth century, is

Palace at Naples, Italy

Long a royal capital, Naples has three royal palaces. The castle rock was once an island, and the body of the siren Parthenope, said to have sung to Ulysses, washed ashore on its beach.

The former royal palace, Athens, Greece

Completed in 1842 for the Danish George I of the Hellenes, the palace now houses the parliament of Greece.

wars, the palace has been well restored. Although it was little used by Greek kings, it has a modestly regal atmosphere, which the more pompous palaces of the time do not achieve.

Belgrade

The royal palace of Serbia in Belgrade was the scene of butchery in 1903 when King Alexander and his queen were shot and hacked to death and their corpses thrown out of the window. The palace itself, built in the late nineteenth century in a fulsome French style, with two little crown-topped domes placed at the corners of the façade like an architect's afterthoughts, still manages to look somewhat nondescript. One critic compared it to the casino of Monte Carlo.

Bucharest

Like Greece, Romania looked to Germany for a king, and chose a branch of the Hohenzollern family. The first king, Carol I (reigned 1881–1914), presided over the modernization of the country; his son Carol II (reigned 1930–40) was more famous for his successive elopements with Zizi Lambrino and Magda Lupescu. But Carol II added many buildings to the capital, Bucharest, including a grand neo-classical

reflected in the turbulent and often violent lives of their rulers. In 1830 the Greek crown was offered to Prince Otto of Bavaria, who was sent packing in 1862 and replaced by a Danish prince, George I of the Hellenes (reigned 1863–1913). Otto had had a palace built in Athens by the Bavarian court architect Friedrich von Gärtner (1792–1847). Finished in 1842 (a year in which his subjects attempted a revolution), the building's austere Germanic interpretation of Greek themes lacks all the subtlety and lightness of the Greek tradition. It is now the Parliament building. George I and his family used its ballroom for cycling and roller-skating.

Corfu

Corfu was one of George I's possessions, given to him by the British government, and with it he inherited a classical palace designed in 1819 by a colonel of the Royal Engineers for the Lord High Commissioner. The palace of St. Michael and St. George is very charming, fitting its setting in a way in which the Athenian one does not. A long Doric arcade forms the ground floor front, flanked by two arches. Inside there is a fine Ionic hall, with a staircase rising to three main rooms, a rotunda, the throne room, with musicians' gallery, and the state dining room. The proportions and craftsmanship are fine. Badly damaged in civil and other

Palace of St. Michael and St. George, Corfu

The charming British-built palace, completed in 1819, was inherited by George I when the British presented him with the island of Corfu.

remodeling of the royal palace in 1930–37. The effect of its oddly articulated façade is undeniably imposing. Inside, there is a great deal of marble and pastiche eighteenth-century decoration. The throne room holds the building's greatest treasure, *The Adoration of the Shepherds* by El Greco, a painter for whom Carol I had a passion (he owned nine works of the master). The palace is now a government building.

Sofia

The royal palace of Bulgaria, in Sofia, now the National Gallery of Art and Ethnography, was originally the Ottoman palace of the Beylerbey. From 1878, when Bulgaria became independent, it was extensively remodeled by German architects for the German kings. The long, rambling building acquired a porte-cochère, an arched pediment, a squared dome, and other Western features in a style that has been referred to as Bulgarian Renaissance. Under King Ferdinand, "Ferdy the Fox" (reigned 1908–18), a large and imposing throne room was inserted on the first floor. Perhaps the most engaging king of Bulgaria was the train-mad Boris III (reigned 1918–43), whose favorite pursuit was driving locomotives on the Bulgarian State Railway.

Tirana

A footnote to these monuments of vanished royalty, standing somewhat forlornly in those eastern capitals, surrounded by the utilitarian constructions of more recently vanished communist dictatorships, is found in the Albanian capital, Tirana. Its monarch from 1928, the irrepressible Ahmed Bey Zogu, or King Zog, transformed it into a town of parks and avenues and set about building himself an appropriate palace. Before he could occupy it, in Easter 1939 the Italians annexed Albania, and Zog fled for the Ritz Hotel in London.

CHAPTER SEVEN

FROM SPAIN TO INDIA:

Palaces of
ISLAM

SPAIN
The Alhambra

In the fourteenth century the domains of the Moors stretched across the Mediterranean Sea and into Spain. In their capital city of Granada, the Nasrid dynasty of caliphs extended the citadel in a series of palatial courtyards to become the Qalat al-Hamra (Palace of Red Walls). On this building was concentrated all the brilliance of the Moorish school. Porcelain tiles, stucco ornament, plasterwork, and paintwork are all combined to give an effect of richness that, ornate as it is, is always controlled and subservient to the overall design. Two superb formal courtyards open into each other and link the halls, with the baths area set between them. The private rooms and the harem area are set behind. The courts and gardens of an Islamic palace are intended to provide a foretaste of Paradise, and the unknown architects achieved a dream-like exquisiteness of style and finish. At the Alhambra, a formal palace intended for show, those who entered its Hall of Ambassadors must have felt they were indeed entering a vision. Nothing in this poetic creation suggests that the rulers who built it were already in retreat, and that at last, in 1492, the last of the caliphs would yield it to the Catholic kings of Aragon and Castile.

The Alhambra, Granada, Spain

From a distance it looks solid and fortress-like: the external view does not prepare the visitor for the richness, delicacy, color, and splendor of the interior of the palace.

The Alhambra, Granada, Spain

Left: The Lion Court, with its slender columns and fretted arches.

Above: Water plays a vital part in creating the ambience of a Moorish palace.

The arches of the Alhambra show the typical stalactite form of Islamic decoration — deep cut hollows resulting in finely shaped pendant shapes that give a sense of delicacy and light. The intricately fretted screens achieve the same feeling. The many different colors of the Alhambra again reveal the architects' genius. Even though almost all the painted decoration is gone, the many colors of stone and marble, the multicolored glass, and brilliant tiles remain to enchant the eye.

Topkapi Palace, Istanbul, Turkey

Above: A general view across the palace and out over the Bosphorus.

Right: The Kiosk of Baghdad, in the northwestern corner of the palace, commemorates the capture of Baghdad by Murat IV in 1638. Shutters and doors are inlaid with tortoiseshell and mother-of-pearl.

TURKEY

Topkapi Palace

Topkapi Saray in Istanbul is one of the world's great palaces, shrouded in legends, the holder of many mysteries, and associated more than anywhere else with the secrets of the harem. Even the names of the various parts of the palace still bring to life the spirit — brilliant, exotic, dangerous — of the long-departed court of the emperor Suleyman I, the Magnificent (reigned 1520–66): the Rooms of the Relics of the Prophet, Halls of the Black and White Eunuchs, the Circumcision Kiosk, the Women's Bath-house, the Jinn's Consultation Hall, the Physician's Tower, and the Executioner's Fountain.

The palace held mosques, libraries, a mint, treasuries, a hospital, schools, an aviary, an indoor pool, gardens, and prisons. Its suite of kitchens could provide meals for 6,000 people. Begun soon after the city had been conquered by Mehmet II, the emperor in 1453, Topkapi was extended, altered, and rebuilt over 500 years. Its name, meaning "cannon gate palace," dates only from the nineteenth century, but the grand plan was laid out between 1459 and 1465, with the harem area reconstructed in 1574–95 and further extended in the seventeenth and eighteenth centuries.

Its many buildings are distributed around four great courts, but the real heart of the palace is the Divan, in the Second Court: three domed rooms, one of which, the Imperial Council Chamber has been restored to its sixteenth-century appearance. In the heart of the main concentration of buildings is the harem, entered from the Courtyard of the Black Eunuchs, a labyrinth of corridors, staircases, and some 300 rooms, with decorative niches, spy-holes, and listening-places, forming an inward-looking little world of voluptuous intrigue and danger.

Topkapi remains an extraordinary treasure-house, with vast collections of jewels, porcelain, armor, illuminated manuscripts, paintings, calligraphy, and silverware. But even if its chambers held nothing but their own domes, niches, arches, and lattices, and their own tiles and frescoes, they would still be among the world's most beautiful rooms.

Fatehpur Sikri, India

Almost contemporary with the early stages of the Topkapi Palace is the palace built by the Mogul emperor Akbar the Great (reigned 1556–1605) at Fatehpur Sikri, India. This remarkable man extended the empire as far as Afghanistan, and he was in many ways one of the most enlightened rulers of the age. His palace-city, built in the local pink-red sandstone of Agra, is a worthy memorial. Like Topkapi, it acted as residence and seat of government. More open in its construction, Fatehpur Sikri is a place of wide courtyards and shady colonnades, with a strong horizontal emphasis, with even the towers built up in wedding-cake tiers. The throne room (Diwan-i-Khass) stands in the center, with the throne itself dramatically placed in the middle of the space, reached by four bridges. Few designs in architecture so clearly convey the solitary nature of imperial rule.

Akbar built a splendid mosque, but, believing that no one faith had a monopoly of wisdom, he constructed a chamber in his palace where scholars of all creeds could share their knowledge. Sadly, they spent so much time in noisy dispute that he closed it.

In the palaces of the Mogul emperors, the sumptuous quality of detail is unsurpassed anywhere. Walls, rather than being decorated with tiles, become elaborate pieces of jewelry on a grand scale, their marble delicately inlaid with precious stones and carved in bas relief. In these buildings, too, the pierced stone screens so typical of Islamic palaces achieve something very close to perfection.

FROM SPAIN TO INDIA: PALACES OF THE ISLAMIC WORLD

Islam spread west and east from the Arab world during the eighth century until Islamic kingdoms, sultanates and empires stretched from the Atlantic to India and central Asia. In southern Spain, Turkey and India, Islamic rulers created palaces of an exquisite beauty and luxury perhaps never seen before. The influence of Islam on art, warfare, architecture and scholarship was enormous and long-lasting.

CHAPTER EIGHT

IMPERIAL

Palaces of the EAST

CHINA
Forbidden City

The "Forbidden City" of Beijing is, in fact, a palace, the imperial government center at the city's heart. The largest architectural complex in China, dating from the early fifteenth century, it is aligned symmetrically north–south and is established according to the geomantic principles of feng-shui. The Forbidden City is a mile (1.6 kilometers) in length and was designed to display the splendor of the emperor as well as to accommodate his court and its different functions. The private court is a traditional feature of Chinese building, and the palace replicates this both in its overall enclosure and in the many courtyards into which it is subdivided. Although a relatively recent building in the long history of China, the strength of tradition both in the use of wood as a building material, and in preserving old-established styles, means that it embodies the Chinese approach to palace-building.

Imperial Palace, Beijing, China

It was under the Qing dynasty that the imperial palace achieved its full size. The great southern gateway, Tian An Men (Gate of Heavenly Peace, erected in 1417) was its main entrance. Within the palace, many other gates controlled entrances to sections, with strict regulations as to who was allowed to use them and when they would be opened. Among the great buildings are the Tai He Dian (Hall of Supreme Harmony, from around 1700) where the Qing emperors transacted the business of state. It stands on a triple terrace of marble at the end of an immense courtyard, and its high double roof, typical of any Chinese dwelling apart from its scale, was designed to daunt those who were allowed to cross towards it.

The emperor was considered to be the Son of Heaven, and his symbol was the dragon. The empress was represented by the phoenix, and a range of other creatures was used to signify power, prosperity, and luck; some of them composite or fantastic creatures like the Qilin, said to symbolize good fortune. Such emblems are everywhere in the palace, as statuary, fountains, or decorative details.

PALACES OF THE ORIENT

The traditions of kingship in ancient Asian lands were influenced by the thousand-year rule of successive emperors of China. Their palaces were built in traditional national styles based on profound respect for the ways in which far-off ancestors had built.

The private rooms of the imperial family are smaller, set around courtyards and fountain-filled rock gardens, with exquisitely cut lattice windows and carved woodwork.

Summer Palace

If the overall effect of the Forbidden City is intentionally daunting, the Summer Palace in Beijing is the complete opposite. Built on the west of the city as a retreat for the Qing emperors, it is a delightful country estate of wooded hills, lakes, walks, and parks, from which pagodas rise, and with delicate bridges arching across the waterways. The names of its parts — Fine Jade Isle, Hill of Longevity, Pavilion of Buddha's Incense, for example — seem to breathe the finest aspects of historic Chinese culture.

Ornamental pavilions form the living accommodation, and there is none of the heavy ceremonial architecture of the forbidden city. It recalls Samuel Taylor Coleridge's vision of Xanadu – the old name given in the West to the capital of China established at Beijing in 1271 by the emperor Kublai Khan (1218-1294):

So twice five miles of fertile ground
With walls and towers were girdled round:
And there were gardens bright with sinuous rills
Where blossom'd many an incense-bearing tree
    –Coleridge, from *Kubla Khan*, 1797

The Forbidden City, Beijing

Below: The strictly compartmentalized layout of the palace can be seen in this general view. Each courtyard was a separate enclave, with its own restrictions as to who might enter; sometimes even the permitted times of entry and exit were set.
Right: The Temple of Heaven

JAPAN

Tokyo

While China has preserved its Imperial Palace only as an historic relic and a continuing symbol of grandeur, the Imperial palaces of Japan are still homes of the emperor. The palace grounds in the center of Tokyo were originally Edo Castle, seat of the Shogun. On the Meiji restoration in 1868, it became the home of the emperor. A nineteenth-century building, it was damaged in the Second World War and rebuilt in 1968. The Imperial Palace in the old capital, Kyoto, is also a modern building, rebuilt in the mid-nineteenth century following a fire in 1788. But the gardens, in their 30-acre (12-hectare) site in the center of the city, are of extreme beauty.

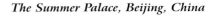

Katsura

A vision of an older Japan and its enduring culture can be seen in the New Palace at Katsura Imperial Villa, built during the seventeenth century by Prince Toshihito and his successor, Prince Toshitada. Japan was then a society of feudal warlords under a military dictatorship, and against this background such exquisite rituals as the tea ceremony evolved. At Katsura, the house and landscape were planned and combined with meticulous taste, using simple and natural materials — wood, stone, rice matting. The structural poles of the villa rest on single stones. Its interior dimensions were determined by the rice mat (shoes, of course, were discarded at the entrance), and the wood of doors and wall paneling was selected and worked with fastidious care, not by elaborate carving but through the selection of graining and natural texture. The design of the garden is ascribed to the tea-master Kobori Enshu.

This deceptively plain and subtle aesthetic was brought to its highest point in houses like Katsura at a time when European princes were covering every inch of their walls with ever-more elaborate plasterwork.

The Summer Palace, Beijing, China

A fanciful pavilion made to resemble a river-boat.

In some of these serene Japanese palaces, however, like the seventeenth-century Nijo Palace in Kyoto, the decorative floral screens of the slightly raised warlord's dais could conceal a lord's room where lurked the bodyguards, armed to the teeth.

CAMBODIA

Far to the south, in the troubled land of Cambodia, a very different palace stands

The Royal Palace, Tokyo, Japan

Above and below: Unlike most city-center palaces, this is an elusive building, hidden in its great green park and showing only occasional glimpses. Nijubashi Bridge, below, may be crossed by the public only on January 2 and December 23, for New Year's Day and the Emperor's Birthday.

Royal Palace, Bangkok, Thailand

Left and above: Built in traditional Thai style, the Royal Palace (c.1780) is a glittering complex of cloisters, temples, and royal apartments.

ruinous in ever-encroaching jungle. This is in Angkor Thom, once the capital of the empire of the Khmers. In 1181, at the age of 50, King Jayavarman VII (reigned 1181–1215/19), having defeated the rival Chams, began to rebuild the city, (whose name simply means "Large City") on a huge scale. The Gate of Victory marks the entrance to his royal palace, set immediately north of the religious center (the king was a pious Buddhist). The royal terraces bound a long rectangular parade ground. From ornate wooden pavilions, the king, seated on a lion skin, and his court would look down at processions, dances, and musical displays. Elephant heads decorated the front of some terraces, and elephants feature largely in the relief sculptures of hunts and battles that adorn the walls. Others are supported by figures of the winged god Garuda, an indication of the godlike nature of the king, since the gods were believed to live in airborne palaces beyond the clouds. Other fine sculptures include the five-headed horse, symbolic of the bodhisattva, or compassionate one; and the strange, solitary, sexless figure known as the Leper King. Unlike many a later palace, that of Angkor Thom had baths, although these stepped

rectangular pools may have been used for ritual, rather than actual physical, cleansing. In the fifteenth century the kings abandoned Angkor Thom for Phnomh Penh; since then the liana, the moss, and the creeper have given the palace and its city the romanticism of decay and forgotten glories.

SOUTH KOREA
Seoul

Back on the Asian mainland, the bustling capital of Seoul still holds the royal palace of Toksu at its center, although no monarch has lived there since the last independent king, Kojong, abdicated in 1907. The palace area is far smaller than Beijing's, but it, too, has its Gate of Heavenly Peace and two main halls, the throne room (Chunghwajon), and the hall of state affairs (Tokongjon). These buildings are in traditional Korean style. On the west side, the Royal Museum is a neo-classical, Western-style building designed by a British architect. With the kind of ironic fate that often seems to

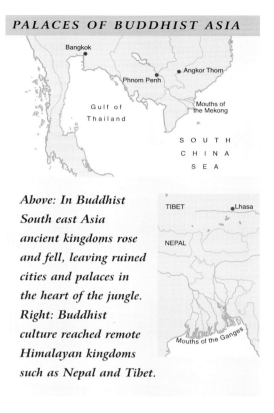

PALACES OF BUDDHIST ASIA

Above: In Buddhist South east Asia ancient kingdoms rose and fell, leaving ruined cities and palaces in the heart of the jungle. Right: Buddhist culture reached remote Himalayan kingdoms such as Nepal and Tibet.

overtake palaces, it was completed in 1909, just before the Japanese takeover ended the long Korean kingship. Now it exhibits mementos of the Yi Dynasty, which ruled Korea from 1392 until the twentieth century.

Potala Palace, Tibet

The golden rooftops of the Potala Palace, Lhasa, Tibet.

TIBET

Potala

Two palaces stand jointly unique in the modern world as centers of both spiritual and temporal rule, although in both cases the temporal rule is a shadow of what it once was. These are the Vatican Palace, center of an independent state in the city of Rome, and the Potala Palace in Lhasa, capital of Tibet, once an independent state and now annexed by China. The Potala, with its principal resident, the Dalai Lama, in exile, scarcely exercises either of its immemorial functions, but it remains a potent symbol of many meanings.

Set in a circle of mountains, the Potala on its rock rises 440 feet (134 meters) above the city of Lhasa, which is spread out before it, and it is 900 feet (275 meters) long. Despite the rocky site, it is a genuine palace, that is, not fortified. The great mass of inward-leaning white-washed buildings seems to grow out of the rock. There has been a palace here since the seventh century, but the present buildings were begun by the fifth Dalai Lama, who died in 1680. It incorporates every aspect of a palace, from the dungeons to the treasure house, said in the 1930s to hold incomparable wealth accumulated as gifts from the Buddhist faithful over the centuries. There is a monastery, a seminary for monks, government offices, rooms of state, and the Dalai Lama's own private apartments. The palace is also a mausoleum, containing the fabulously ornate tombs of his predecessors. F. Spencer Chapman, a British visitor in the 1930s, was critical of the interior: "True, there are certain details — a painting on the wall, a golden butter-lamp, or even a complete room, which are worthy of the palace — but there is no sort of unity; and the various assembly halls, shrines, and storerooms are connected by dark and evil-smelling passages slippery with the spillings of innumerable cups of Tibetan tea, while the whole place is anything but clean."

In the audience rooms, frescoes, almost invisible in the gloom, were observed, with tall pillars swathed in cloth, and silk banners hanging from smoke-blackened ceilings. High on the flat roof-tops, gilded turrets and pavilions rise, along with cylindrical banners of black and white yak-hair, whose function is to keep devils at bay. Even under present conditions, the Potala remains a truly extraordinary palace.

The Potala Palace, Lhasa, Tibet

The lower buildings are known as the White Palace, while the Dalai Lamas' living quarters and tombs are in the upper area, the Red Palace. The name of the Potala comes from a site in the far south of India — seat of the bodhisattva Avalokitesvara, patron deity of Tibet.

CHAPTER NINE

THE
Magnificent
MAHARAJAHS

As the Mogul Empire of India fell into decline, bands of military adventurers roamed across the subcontinent and the most successful began to set up their own kingdoms, initially still under the aegis of the emperor. These were the Rajputs. When the British took control of India, they incorporated these princely states into their empire, and so began the era of the Maharajahs. In a land whose typical dwelling was the one-roomed hut, the rulers were to create palaces whose style varies enormously, but whose keynote is opulence and swagger. Descendants of warriors, the rulers of India were also the subjects of Queen Victoria, and their palaces combine the exercise of semi-medieval power with the amenities of the English country mansion.

Palace of the Winds, Jaipur, India

The Hawa Mahal, "Palace of the Winds," rises above the old main street of Jaipur. Built in 1799 by Maharajah Sawai Pratap Singh, the five-story pink sandstone structure was intended to be lived in by the ladies of the royal household. From its finely carved window-frames, they could look down and observe all that went on in the world outside.

Jaipur

At Jaipur is one of the earliest princely palaces, founded in 1728 by Jai Singh II. It brings together elements of Mogul palace architecture with Hindu influences. The layout, with the separate functions clearly set apart, is Mogul, as are the refined details of style. In the open, pavilion-like form of Jaipur, notably two audience halls and the guest house (Mubarak Mahal), the influence of Fatehpur Sikri (see pages 84–5) can be seen. But the seclusion of the Chandra Mahal (Moon Palace), together with its ornamentation of lotus flower and spear-head, show the Hindu tradition.

Bundi

The British observer Lieutenant-Colonel Tod said in 1820 that, of the many palaces of Rajasthan, the unquestionably preeminent one was the palace of Bundi. The walls rise steep on a mountain slope above the town. In fact, it is a series of palaces, of which the largest and most remarkable was built in the early eighteenth century by Chatar Sal, using greenish serpentine, a fine-grained sandstone. Elephant symbols are everywhere, and although there is some lavish Mogul design, this palace is more emphatically Hindu in style, with decorative brackets supporting balconies and ceilings, and disguising the arches. The many levels of Bundi were compared by Tod to the fabulous Hanging Gardens of Babylon.

The City Palace, Jaipur, India

Left: Set in the heart of the old city, a congeries of courtyards, gardens, and buildings. The palace area includes the "suttee wall," where the wives who burned themselves to death on their dead husband's funeral pyres are commemorated.

Above: A detail of carving.

PALACES OF THE MAHARAJAHS

In India, princely states ruled by wealthy maharajahs came into being around the end of the eighteenth century. Allied with the British raj, they lost power after India gained independence.

Remote from the main arteries of India, Bundi, more than 240 miles (390 kilometers) from Delhi, preserved its own traditional approach. It had a water clock, with a bowl that took an hour to fill and an attendant whose job it was to strike a gong as the water reached the rim. Umed Singh (reigned 1744–71), was the patron of the Bundi school of Indian art, and he is responsible for the Chitra Shala (art gallery) with its strikingly executed paintings of religious and mythological scenes, hunts and battles.

Baroda

Like Gwalior, the state of Baroda (now Vadodara) emerged from the Maratha military expansion of the eighteenth century. Pilaji Gaekwad captured Baroda in 1734; it was the center of a rich territory and became one of the largest princely states. There were few changes until Sayajirao III acceded in 1881 at the age of 12, and proceeded to introduce the modern world. His Laxmi Vilmas Palace was completed in 1890 after 12 years, designed by the brilliant but neurotic Major Mont

(who became convinced all his buildings would fall down). The palace is remarkable for its ornate wells.

Baroda's wealth was expressed in fine craftsmanship. At the Exhibition of Indian Art in Delhi in 1903, the Baroda Pearl Carpet was a center of attention: pearls, diamonds, rubies, and emeralds were incorporated into its design. A few decades earlier, a priceless veil was made in Baroda, to be offered as a covering for the tomb of the Prophet Mohammed at Medina.

The City Palace, Jaipur, India

Above: the "Peacock Door."

The Amber Palace, Jaipur, India

Right: Many-columned hall with false arches.

City Palace of Gwalior, India

The Scindia family of Gwalior arose after the Mogul decline, coming north from Maharashtra and establishing themselves here. The central feature of a Maharajah's palace is his Durbar Hall, originally intended for giving audience to his Indian subjects, but also used for ceremonial meetings with his British "advisers." Maharajah Jayaji Rao built the City Palace in Gwalior between 1872 and 1874, to the designs of a British army engineer, Sir Michael Filose. The external effect, despite vast quantities of white marble, is not very distinguished, but the interior is grandiose. The two three-ton chandeliers of the Durbar Hall are said to be the biggest in the world. Its walls and doors are painted with gold leaf, and gold thread is woven into the heavy brocade curtains. The rooms are very Italianate, with much use of glass, even glass banisters and furniture. On the death of Jayaji Rao, a vast hoard of wealth was found hidden in the palace, which enabled his successor, Madhav Rao, to own race-horses and operate his own private railway. A smaller train, made of silver, moved round his enormous dinner table to circulate the cigars and port.

Described as "the most wonderful piece of embroidery ever known," its arabesques of costly thread and jewels cost 10 million rupees. It was never sent.

Morvi

In northwest India, on the Kathiawad Peninsula where Krishna is believed to have lived and died, is the small state of Morvi. Between 1879 and 1948 it was ruled by Waghji, who introduced roads, railways, and

Laxmi Vilmas Palace, Baroda, India

Built of red sandstone and blue trapstone, it is divided into the traditional three zones of a Hindu palace – the public rooms with the great hall, the Maharajah's rooms, and the zenana, or women's area – but it incorporates many Western innovations, including a billiards room. It is a palace on a considerable scale, with a frontage 500 feet (152 meters) long, and done in a grand amalgam of styles. The public apartments are Mogul in appearance; the Maharajah seems to occupy a Hindu fort, and the women's area is a riot of domes and spirelets to rival St. Mark's in Venice. The interior is opulently European.

electricity. He built a palace in 1931–44, only a few years before the power of the princes would be engulfed by the new Republic of India.

Long and low, with a modest central block, the palace is one of the great monuments of late Art Deco. Its outer appearance could be that of an office building, and its smooth granite is often taken to be reinforced concrete. Inside, it has splendid details—decorative arches, niches, fountains and baths—in which the angularity of Art Deco acquires a curvaceous playfulness. There are six drawing rooms, six dining rooms, some with the original tubular furniture, a swimming pool, a card room, and a billiards room. There is a harking back to an older Indian tradition in the erotic murals of a bedroom suite.

Patiala

The biggest of Indian palaces is the Old Motibagh Palace of Patiala, the largest Sikh princedom of the Punjab. Perhaps more than any other, it epitomizes the ostentation of the Maharajahs. Its most notable inhabitant, Bhupinder Singh, was a larger-than-life figure, reputed to have some 90 children. The palace covers 11 acres (4.5 hectares). Built of rose-colored sandstone, it spreads along a vast frontage but also extends back from the central block into a huge central area, which rises to a dome set well back from the façade. Lesser domes, finials, crockets, and spirelets punctuate the roof-line. Fifteen dining rooms are provided, and the Durbar Hall has 100 chandeliers. Everything was on the grand scale, not least

the Sheesh Mahal, or Hall of Mirrors. In the grounds of the palace, Bhupinder Singh had a zoo. He owned 72 automobiles, of which 36 were Rolls-Royces.

Cooch-Behar

Cooch-Behar is tiger and elephant country, in the far northeast of India, and here, in savanna country, overlooking wide lawns and a lily-filled lake, is to be found a dome modeled on St. Peter's in Rome. It is the dominating feature of the palace, which was built in the late nineteenth century in Italian Renaissance style by the Maharajah Nripendra Narain and his independent-spirited wife, Sunity Devee. It is a handsome building, although its red-brick exterior

Vice-regal, now Presidential, Palace, Delhi, India

The British, who ruled India until 1948, originally did so from Calcutta, but in 1911 the capital was moved to Delhi. Perhaps stimulated by the example of the Maharajahs, the colonial administration built a palace in Delhi for the Viceroy that was the grandest of all – and much more imposing than the king-emperor's own palace in London. The Vice-regal, now Presidential, Palace has two fronts, each 600 feet (183 meters) in length, and its dome is 180 feet (55 meters) high. Covering 4.5 acres (1.8 hectares) and with 11 courtyards, built of blood-red and cream sandstone, it is on the scale of the great European palaces. The architect was Sir Edwin Lutyens (1869–1944), who skillfully fused the proportions and outlines of Europe with the colors, water effects, and details of Mogul India. The palace's Durbar Hall is of white marble with a porphyry floor and columns of yellow jasper in its four apses. The palace was completed in 1929. Less than 20 years later, in 1948, it became the property of the Republic of India, but the scarlet-clad horse-guards still keep watch from its stone sentry boxes.

seems more municipal than palatial. Inside the palace, however, luxury takes over. Elephant tusks and trophy heads on the walls recall the favorite pastime of former occupants, although the yellow and pink drawing rooms, with their Chippendale-style mirrors and tables, seem far from forest or jungle.

CHAPTER TEN

THE UNITED STATES:

From Enlightenment to
PLUTOCRACY

There is still a real palace in the United States. A mansion of modest size in the center of Washington, D.C., the White House carries out all the historic functions that the palace has had since earliest times. It is the chief citizen's office as well as his home, and from it a power is wielded that imperial rulers like Sargon or Philip II could never have imagined. When it was built, in 1793–81, the United States had more to be modest about. The Irish-born architect, James Hoban (*c*.1762–1831), designed a handsome and graceful house in the Palladian style, with a bold but not showy bow-shaped portico whose tall columns rise through two stories. In its early days, it dominated the little city. As an official residence, owned by the state, the White House interior has a certain impersonality, despite the traces of various Presidential households. One individual cannot make a mark upon it, as Thomas Jefferson (1743–1826) did at Monticello, Virginia, but Jefferson's Palladian mansion, for all its interest, is not a palace.

The White House, Washington, D.C.

Handsomely executed by James Hoban (c.1762–1831), the White House is restrained and modest in scale, in tribute to the democratic ideals of the Founding Fathers.

The White House, Washington, D.C.

The Greek Revival portico identifies the White House firmly as an architectural expression of the Age of Reason, the great period of republican ideals.

Biltmore

At Asheville, North Carolina, George W. Vanderbilt (1862–1914) erected Biltmore, a vast chateau in the French Renaissance style. Designed by Richard Morris Hunt (1827–95) and built between 1890 and 1895, its inspiration came from the Loire castles of Blois, Chambord, and Chenonceaux. But Biltmore does not have the symmetry of a Chambord; it is more Gothic in feeling. Its walls are of fine-grained Indiana limestone, carved only around the windows, but the grand entrance pavilion is flamboyant, with a pierced stone parapet and an array of dormer windows, pinnacles, finials, and little flying buttresses. Its frontage is 780 feet (238 meters) long, and at the rear a massive retaining wall 75 feet (23 meters) high compensates for the natural slope of its site.

Biltmore, Asheville, North Carolina

Above: An external view.

Right: The banqueting hall.

Inside there are 250 rooms, throbbing with color and detail. A palm court with fountains leads to the great stair hall, from which a staircase of white marble with a bronze banister rises. Perhaps the finest room is the banqueting hall, with its triple fireplace at one end and the organ gallery at the other. Above the fireplace is a neo-classical stone frieze by the Austrian-born sculptor Karl Bitter (1867–1915). This hall of an uncrowned king of industry actually does boast two carved Gothic thrones. Its lofty walls are decorated by stags' heads and

Biltmore, Asheville, North Carolina

The Library, showing the staircase and gallery.

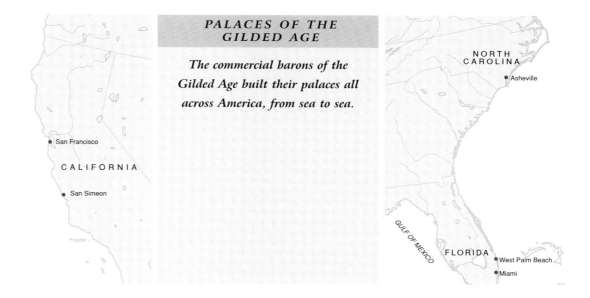

PALACES OF THE GILDED AGE

The commercial barons of the Gilded Age built their palaces all across America, from sea to sea.

banners, with high windows rising to the arched, wood-beamed roof. There are splendid Persian and Kurdistan rugs. The Tapestry Gallery was built to show three fine sixteenth-century tapestries and a collection of royal Dresden porcelain. The Library is another imposing room, paneled in walnut, with a gallery reached by an elaborate spiral staircase. Its ceiling shows a vast painting attributed to the eighteenth-century Italian artist Giovanni Antonio Pellegrini (1675–1741).

The private rooms are not reticent. In Mr. Vanderbilt's bedroom, the canopied bed seems quite small, set among marble panels carved in relief and ornate eighteenth-century furniture. It is a Victorian-Jacobean room, while Mrs. Vanderbilt's is a grand exercise in restrained rococo, with yellow silk walls between dado and cornice, fragile furniture, a curvily sculptured fireplace, and gold-framed portraits of royalty. Among the many treasures of Biltmore are a velvet wall-

hanging of Cardinal Richelieu's, Napoleon's chess-table, and rare Chinese bronzes.

Outside, Frederick Law Olmsted (1822–1903) laid out a park and formal garden to complement the house, with terraces, box hedges, flower beds, walks, and fountains, populated by stone fauns, goddesses, and cherubs. A half-mile vista was opened through the woodland beyond.

Whitehall

Henry Morrison Flagler (1830–1913) selected a different epoch for his palace, Whitehall, in Palm Beach, Florida, and chose as his architects John Merven Carrère (1858–1911) and Thomas Hastings (1860–1929), designers of the U.S. Senate. A high portico of Roman-Doric pillars runs for two-thirds of the length of the house, with a coffered ceiling, and displaying every classical dentil and modillion in its frieze and cornice. The chimneys, linked by bracing walls, become decorative features.

At enormous expense, the finest craftsmen were summoned from France and Italy to work on the house, whose rooms range in style from French, Spanish, and Swiss to English and colonial American. The marble hall measures 110 by 40 feet (34 x 12 meters), with an enormous fresco in its dished ceiling, said to celebrate "The Coming of Knowledge."

There is an assembly hall for lectures and concerts, and the music room, in Louis XIV style, had the largest organ of any private house. Gold-threaded damask acts as a background to the fine paintings hanging in this room. The ballroom is a grand expanse of gilt and glass, with eighteenth-century panel paintings of the seasons by François Boucher (1703–70). The satinwood dining room is in the style of that great French palace-builder, François I. Flagler was another zealous collector, as keen to install a fifth-century Byzantine font as he was to extend his range of French paintings.

Casa Grande

The scenic beauty, secluded woodland, and mild climate of the California coastline around San Simeon made it William Randolph Hearst's favorite place on earth. He was already immensely wealthy when he began to build his Casa Grande, constantly harassing his architect, Julia Morgan (1872–1957), with new demands and adaptations. The palace takes many elements from different times and cultures and welds them into its own unique scheme.

Fronted like a Roman basilica, the house is flanked by Spanish Renaissance bell-towers, each holding a full carillon of bells. The 100-

Casa Grande, San Simeon, California

Right: The swimming pool. Compare Hadrian's garden at Tivoli on page 18.

Below left: The bell-towers of the façade.

room interior held Roman mosaics, Persian and Turkish carpets, Flemish tapestries, Italian chimney breasts, Chinese vases, and paintings from the world's art traditions in a single immense collection.

Hearst entertained on the grand scale, and his guests mingled in the assembly room, into which he descended to meet them, before moving to the Refectory, a baronial hall with Sienese banners, a sixteenth-century Italian carved ceiling, Gothic choir stalls, and Flemish tapestries. Despite these period features, Casa Grande is also a twentieth-century palace, with movie theater, beauty parlor, a private airfield, and garaging for a fleet of automobiles.

There are the outdoor Neptune Pool, with a colonnade reminiscent of Hadrian's Villa, and the guest "cottages," each of 10 to 18 rooms, where visitors, often movie stars, stayed for fancy-dress parties and enormous picnics. Hearst also had a zoo laid out. On one occasion, woken at dead of night in her sumptuous apartment by the howling of orangutans, the lady of the house said: "The whole place is crazy." Casa Grande was lived in from 1925 to 1951; it is now owned by the state of California.

CHAPTER ELEVEN

ENDPIECE:

Modern PALACES

The palace is above all the visible symbol of monarchy. Every republic has its presidential palace, but the president is only a tenant, occupying the house at the will of the people for a limited time. In the case of a king or queen, the monarch is the owner. Not only is the palace theirs for life: it is their family property, passing to their descendants. Dictators, as self-appointed monarchs, but without the security of tradition and heredity, are usually even more keen to display their status. Tragic countries, like the Central African Republic, under its self-proclaimed Emperor Bokassa, saw vast building schemes while the population went hungry. Grandly palatial building plans were a favorite pastime of Adolf Hitler. During the communist period, dictators such as Nicolae Ceaucescu in Romania erected grandiose "People's Palaces" like great termitaries, which most people were forbidden to enter.

Sultan's Palace, Bandar Seri Begawan, Brunei

The Ruler of Brunei, one of the world's smallest countries, is one of the world's richest men. His new palace is an ambitious attempt to bring traditional styles of Islamic architecture and design together with the latest constructional technology. Despite its austere, linear, undecorated external appearance, it is opulently decorated inside. The view from the antechamber through to the throne room (right), and the throne room itself (left), show that the aim of emphasizing personal sovereignty is every bit as clear as it was at Knossos. No expense was spared in the decorating of the building, within the guidelines of Islamic art. As one indication of this, the domes are gilded with 22 carat gold leaf (see page 115).

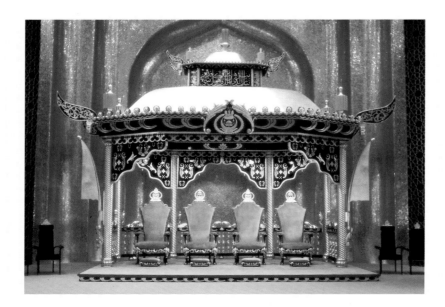

The People's Palace, Bucharest, Romania

This style of architecture, a kind of pared-down classicism, was first seen in Moscow in the Stalinist 1930s, and it rapidly became the official style throughout the Soviet empire. Looked at objectively, some of these structures have a certain dignity of mass and proportion, but is it impossible to forget their overall function, which, like the architecture of Nazi Germany, was to exalt the power of the state and stifle the identity of the individual. The lack of feature and detail was not just a stylistic whim of the architects (often committees, not single designers): it intentionally turned its back on the humanistic scale created centuries before by the Greek orders.

The twentieth century, with a wider range of governmental styles than any previous one, saw no reduction in the rate of palace construction. The geographical focus shifted from Europe and the West to the Middle and Far East, where kingdoms and princely states were still often ruled on an autocratic basis, and great wealth from oil revenues encouraged conspicuous expenditure.

The prime example in recent years, and one that any visitor may enter, is the new palace of the tiny Sultanate of Brunei, near the eastern tip of Borneo. This oil-rich state is ruled by one of the world's richest men, and his palace, for all its ultra-modern architecture and high-tech materials, is a fascinating example of how little has changed in the display of power and authority through the centuries. The palace remains an enduring institution that has survived millennia of human history. It is safe to predict that it will be with us for a long time to come.

Sultan's Palace, Bandar Seri Begawan, Brunei

The palace, built in only three years between 1980 and 1983, thanks to the use of modern materials like reinforced concrete, is formally known as the Istana Nurul Iman. The palace has 1788 rooms. Its great banqueting hall can hold 4000 guests, although the royal dining room, with space for 500, is also used for more intimate functions. The Surau (prayer hall) is another vast inner space capable of holding 1500 worshipers.

GLOSSARY

Architrave The main beam resting above a line of columns, a doorway, or window.

Baroque A post-Renaissance style of architecture and interior decoration, notable for lush carving and dramatic effects.

Basilica A high, rectangular hall, with aisles at each side, separated from the main hall by rows of columns

Bas-relief A sculptural effect in which the shape stands out only slightly from the surface.

Capital The decoratively carved block at the top of a column.

Colonnade A roofed walkway supported by columns.

Cornice The molding that completes the top of a wall, either inside or outside.

Crocket A decorative projection, often a ball of carved foliage, on a Gothic structure.

Cupola A dome.

Dado The lower part of a wall, given separate decorative treatment from the rest of the surface.

Dentils Regular series of small, square block shapes, forming part of the design of Ionic and Corinthian cornices.

Dormer window A window built into a sloping roof, often with a miniature pitched roof of its own, set at right angles to the main roof-line.

Entablature In classical architecture, the superstructure resting above the columns.

Finial A final detail of stone or metal set on the top of a spire or pitched roof.

Flying buttress An arched or angled wall support built separately from the wall and joining it at the end of the arch.

Frieze A horizontal band of sculpture.

Fresco A painting applied directly to the damp plaster surface of a wall.

Gothic A style of architecture defined by the use of pointed arches.

Hammer-beam roof A timber roof built up on a series of massive wooden brackets, each supporting the one above.

Intarsia Designs or images created with inlaid woodwork.

Light-well A space left open to the sky in the interior of a building, to allow light to fall into the inner parts.

Linenfold paneling Carved wood panels that give a visual effect resembling folded sheets of linen.

Loggia An open gallery, usually colonnaded, that can be set in an upper wall or be at ground level.

Mausoleum A building intended to house a tomb or tombs.

Modillion A decorative bracket, usually in a scroll form, supporting a cornice.

Monolith A pillar made of a single block of stone.

Palladian In the style of Andrea Palladio (1508–80).

Parterre A formally arranged decorative flowerbed.

Pediment The triangular, gable-like structure crowning the end of a Greek temple, or the portico of a palace.

Piano nobile The principal floor of a palace, where the main public rooms are to be found.

Pilaster An imitation column built into the surface of a wall.

Porphyry A hard crystalline rock, which takes a very high polish.

Porte-cochère A high porch built out from the front door of a great house, leaving enough space for a carriage to drive in beneath its roof, sheltering passengers from the weather.

Portico The colonnaded space in front of a main entrance.

Putti Sculptures or paintings of cherub-like infant boys.

Pylon The massive, pyramidal-shaped entrance to an Egyptian temple or palace.

Relief Sculpture on a panel, where the sculptured design is raised above the surface.

Rococo A theatrical and highly decorative approach to design, a continuation of baroque.

Rustication A building style used for the lower parts of palaces, using massive stone blocks with deeply incised spaces between them, and the surfaces usually roughened.

Stucco A smooth covering applied to the outer faces of brick or stone walls; a thick paste that dries very hard and can be shaped into different designs, or painted.

Topiary Cutting of hedges and close-leaved trees into ornamental shapes.

Tribune A gallery above the aisle in a hall or church.

Trompe l'oeil A form of painting that deceives the eye with a false perspective.

FURTHER READING

Acton, Harold. *The Bourbons of Naples*. London: Methuen, 1956

Arthaud, Claude. *Dream Palaces*. London: Thames & Hudson, 1973

Bence-Jones M. *Palaces of the Raj*. London: Allen & Unwin, 1958

Borsook, Eve. *Companion Guide to Florence*. London: Collins, 1974

Braham, A. and Smith, P. *François Mansart*. London: Zwemmer, 1973

Bussagli, M. *Oriental Architecture*. New York: Abrams, 1973

Cadogan, Gerald. *Palaces of the Minoan Crete*. London: Barrie & Jenkins, 1976

Carandente, G. *Rome*. London: Thames & Hudson, 1971

Dodds, J.D. *Al-Andalus: Art of Islamic Spain*. New York, Metropolitan Museum, 1972

Fatesinghrao, Gaekwad. *Palaces of India*. London: Collins, 1980

Godfrey, F.M. *Italian Architecture up to 1750*. London: Alec Tiranti, 1967

Godwin, Godfrey. *History of Ottoman Architecture*. London: Thames & Hudson, 1971

Hamilton, G.H. *Art and Architecture of Russia*. London: Penguin, 1954

Hayden, B. and Gendrop, P. *Pre-Columbian Architecture of Meso-America*. New York: Abrams, 1975

Hitchcock, Henry-Russell. *Architecture: Nineteenth and Twentieth Centuries*. London & New York: Penguin

Kennet, Audrey. *Palaces of Leningrad*. London: Debrett, 1973

Montague-Smith, Patrick, and Montgomery - Massingberd, Hugh, *Royal Palaces, Castles and Homes*. London: Debrett, 1981

Lloyd, H., Muller, H.W., and Martin, R. *Ancient Architecture*. New York: Abrams, 1979

Macaulay, Rose. *The Pleasure of Ruins*. London: Thames & Hudson, 1953

Morris, James. *Venice*. London: Faber & Faber, 1960

Sitwell, Sacheverell. *Great Palaces*. London: Weidenfeld & Nicolson, 1964

Smith, E.W. *Moghul Architecture of Fatehpur-Sikhri*. Government Press, Allahabad, 1894

Sumner-Boyd, Hilary and Freely, John. *Strolling Through Istanbul*. London & New York: KPI, 1967

Thorndike, J. *The Magnificent Builders*. London: Paul Elek, 1978

Watkin, David. *A History of Western Architecture*. London: Laurence King, 1986

Welch, Stuart. *India: Art and Culture, 1300–1900*. New York: Metropolitan Museum, 1985

Williams, H.L. and O. *Great Houses of America*. London: Weidenfeld & Nicolson, 1967

INDEX

INDEX

PHOTO CREDITS

The Publisher wishes to thank the following picture agencies for supplying pictures for inclusion in this work. All reasonable efforts have been made to provide accurate credits and acknowledgements.

Austrian National Tourist Office: 8/9, 10/11

Biltmore Estate, Ashville, USA: Courtesy of the Biltmore Estate, Ashville: 106L, 106/107, 108

J Allan Cash Ltd: 6 and 80, 16, 17, 22L, 60T, 75, 78/79

CFCL/ISI: 56, 57, 65, 69, 72, 81, 84/85, 86, 86/87, 88, 89, 90/91, 94/95, 98/99, 99R

Corel CD-ROM: 2, 66, 92T, 92B, 97

Dinodia Picture Agency: 100L, 101, 102T, 102B, 103

Farabolafoto: 34

Foto Majrani: 74

German National Tourist Office: 70, 70/71

Giraudon: 5, 23, 36 (Giraudon/Alinari), 37, 48, 49, 50/51

Image Select: 20/21

J S Library International: 85, 100R, 112, 113, 115T, 115B

NIS-Photo Archives of the Netherlands Government Information Service: Osterreich Werbung: 67

PIX: 12, 13, 60B, 83 (De Laubier), 18 (Lescourret), 22 (Guiziou), 24/25, 41T, 41B, 42/43, 44/45, 73, 76 (Dusart), 27, 29 (Silberstein), 38/39 (Benazat), 40 (Moes), 46 (Miriski), 46/47, 55, 58/59, 68 (Price), 104, 105

Rex Features: 82, 114 (Sean Longden)

Royal Collection Enterprises Ltd: by graceful permission of HRH The Queen: 53T (Mark Fiennes)

Royal Collections, Stockholm: 61

Spectrum Colour Library: 15, 33, 42, 50, 52, 53B, 63R, 91TR, 91BR, 93, 110L, 110/111

Telegraph Colour Library: 62/63

Trip: 77 (Bognar)

Werner Forman Archive: 19, 30

Picture Research by Alex Goldberg and Letty Savonitto of Image Select International Ltd.